FIX-IT and FORGET-IT®
slow-cooker magic

at your service

Please direct comments or questions about *Fix-It and Forget-It® Slow-Cooker Magic* to:

Good Books
E-mail **custserv@GoodBooks.com** or write:
Good Books
3510 Old Philadelphia Pike
P.O. Box 419
Intercourse, PA 17534

Interested in more Oxmoor House books?
Find a wide variety of titles from your favorite brands—*Southern Living, Cooking Light, Williams-Sonoma,* and many more! Whether you enjoy cooking, gardening, or decorating, you'll find a wealth of how-to books that can be shipped straight to your door. Please visit **oxmoorhouse.com** for our many special offers, or call 1-800-491-0551.

To search, savor, and share thousands of recipes, visit **myrecipes.com**

FIX-IT AND FORGET-IT® SLOW-COOKER MAGIC is published by Oxmoor House, Inc., Book Division of Southern Progress Corporation, P.O. Box 2262, Birmingham, Alabama 35201-2262.

ISBN-13: 978-0-8487-3209-7
ISBN-10: 0-8487-3209-X

FIX-IT and FORGET-IT®
slow-cooker magic

EDITOR	Elizabeth Taliaferro
PROJECT EDITOR	Julie Boston
SENIOR DESIGNER	Melissa Jones Clark
COPY CHIEF	L. Amanda Owens

OXMOOR HOUSE SPECIAL EDITIONS

VP, PUBLISHER	Brian Carnahan
EDITOR IN CHIEF	Nancy Fitzpatrick Wyatt
EXECUTIVE EDITOR	Susan Carlisle Payne
ART DIRECTOR	Keith McPherson
MANAGING EDITOR	Allison Long Lowery
DIRECTOR OF PRODUCTION	Laura Lockhart
DIRECTOR, TEST KITCHENS	Elizabeth Tyler Austin
ASSISTANT DIRECTOR, TEST KITCHENS	Julie Christopher
TEST KITCHENS PROFESSIONALS	Jane Chambliss; Patricia Michaud; Kathleen Royal Phillips; Catherine Crowell Steele; Ashley T. Strickland; Kate Wheeler, R.D.
PHOTOGRAPHY DIRECTOR	Jim Bathie
SENIOR PHOTO STYLIST	Kay E. Clarke
ASSOCIATE PHOTO STYLIST	Katherine G. Eckert
SENIOR PRODUCTION MANAGER	Greg A. Amason
PRODUCTION MANAGER	Theresa Beste-Farley
CONTRIBUTORS	Rick Soldin (compositor); Jasmine Hodges (copy editor); Lauren Brooks (proofreader); Anne-Harris Jones, Erin Loudy, Shea Staskowski, Lauren Wiygul (interns); Beau Gustafson, Lee Harrelson (photographers); Melanie J. Clarke (photo stylist); Debby Maugans, Ana Price Kelly (food stylists)

GOOD BOOKS

PUBLISHER	Merle Good
SENIOR BOOK EDITOR	Phyllis Pellman Good

SOUTHERN PROGRESS CORPORATION

PRESIDENT AND CEO	Tom Angelillo
EXECUTIVE VICE PRESIDENTS	Bruce Akin, Jeanetta Keller, Bruce Larson, Scott Sheppard
VP, ADMINISTRATION	Lane Schmitt
VP, CONSUMER MARKETING	Steve Crowe
VP, PRODUCTION	Randy Lavies
VP, TECHNOLOGY	Brett Steele

cover: Italian Country Pork, page 65
left: Peanut Butter Cake, page 106

welcome!

Dear Cooking Friend,

Home-cooked meals fuel our bodies, and the time we spend together with family and friends is priceless. If you are searching for simple recipes for your busy lifestyle that will please your family or result in mouthwatering main dishes fit for company, you've picked up the right cookbook.

Preparing meals in the slow cooker is one of the best ways to turn mealtime into a pleasant repast. Preparation is simple and quick, and you can fix a recipe when you're not distracted or feeling pressured. Besides having a delicious meal ready when they arrive home, the millions of *Fix-It and Forget-It*® fans agree that the rich aroma that greets them at dinnertime says welcome home like nothing else.

Fix-It and Forget-It® Slow-Cooker Magic **offers an all-new collection of recipes that fit your schedule precisely.** One thing I know for certain is that our lives are busier than ever before and the time we have to cook is limited. That's why we've designed the first half of the book according to the time these recipes take to slow-cook. And these recipes have only five ingredients not including salt, pepper, all-purpose flour, cornstarch, oil, water, and optional ingredients. Try a soon-to-be-favorite such as Quick and Easy Mushroom Brisket (page 13), Scalloped Potatoes and Ham (page 25), Hearty Lentil and Sausage Stew (page 34), or Pizza Fondue (page 47). Whether you're looking for a recipe that slow-cooks while you're out of the house for a few hours or while you're gone the entire day, you'll find plenty that are easy to assemble and certain to be ready to eat when you get home.

Of course, you'll discover multiple main-dish recipes that are perfect for the family, plus all sorts of other recipes surprisingly prepared in the slow cooker. Try such dessert favorites as Chocolate Bread Pudding (page 104), irresistible appetizers for entertaining like Red Pepper and Feta Toasts (page 55), and traditional side dishes such as Green Beans Au Gratin (page 97).

I hope that the recipes in *Fix-It and Forget-It® Slow-Cooker Magic* give you just what you'll need to prepare wholesome foods for family and friends at your convenience and on your schedule. **After all, it's important for everyone to enjoy mealtime, especially the cook!**

Happy Slow Cooking!

Phyllis Pellman Good

Phyllis Pellman Good

page 25

page 87

contents

page 67

slow-cooker cookbook

page 85

all about slow cooking

Simplify day-to-day living with *Fix-It and Forget-It® Slow-Cooker Magic* and these handy tips and techniques.

slow cookers and features

Slow cookers have come a long way since they were introduced in the 1970s. The long slow cooking times that added a distinct depth of flavor, as well as the ability to leave cooking food unattended, made slow cookers a fast success story. But like all kitchen appliances, improved manufacturing, technology, and fashion trends over the years have resulted in more efficient and stylish slow cookers.

• New slow cookers tend to cook faster than older models, so if you haven't bought one in a while, you might want to start shopping.

• Slow cookers come in a variety of sizes—from 1 quart to 7 quarts, with half-sizes in between—as well as in round and oval shapes.

• Newer slow cookers are available in decorator colors including candy-apple red, white, black, and stainless.

• Cookers with removable inserts make for easier cleanup compared with one-piece units. Some models' inserts are dishwasher safe.

• Preset cook cycles for foods often slow-cooked, such as chili or pot roast, are popular. Once the setting is chosen, the cooker tracks the food's temperature and knows when it's done.

• Slow-cooker inserts that can go from freezer to slow cooker are becoming popular. Some are even safe for browning meat directly on the cooktop.

• An external timer device, sold separately for older slow-cooker models, allows you to set the cook time; when the time has expired, the timer automatically switches the cooker to warm. Simply plug your cooker into the timer, and then plug the timer into the wall outlet.

• Some cookers now have a base that doubles as a griddle.

• Other extras include automatic on/off switch, programmable models with digital timers, dual cookers that allow an entrée and side dish to cook simultaneously, retractable cords, and accessories like cooking racks, baking inserts, and insulated carrying totes.

slow-cooker safety

• When cooking raw meats and poultry, the U.S. Department of Agriculture recommends using high heat for the first hour to make sure ingredients reach a safe temperature quickly. Then you can reduce the heat to low for the remainder of the cooking time.

• You can omit the high heat for the first hour in recipes that brown the meat first, since precooking jump-starts the initial temperature of ingredients.

• Cut a whole chicken or pieces of meat larger than 3 pounds in half before placing them in the slow cooker. This allows the slow cooker to heat up faster and the heat to penetrate the meat more easily and destroy any bacteria.

• Defrost any frozen foods before cooking to make sure the contents of the crock reach a safe temperature quickly.

• Always fill a slow cooker at least halfway full and no more than two-thirds full in order for food to reach a safe temperature and cook evenly throughout.

• Use the specified slow-cooker size to ensure proper levels of food, thorough cooking, and safe temperatures. If your slow cooker is a different size than the recipe recommends, adjust the cooking time accordingly.

• All cooked foods, including slow-cooked foods, should be eaten or refrigerated within 2 hours to prevent bacteria growth.

• Minute for minute, the slow cooker and a 75-watt light bulb use about the same amount of electricity, which is much less than a conventional oven.

ingredient essentials

• Pasta retains the best texture when cooked separately and according to package directions. Add cooked pasta to the slow cooker during the last 30 minutes of cooking unless otherwise directed.

• Long grain converted rice is best in recipes that call for cooking rice in the slow cooker.

• Dried beans take longer to tenderize if combined with sugar and acid. To achieve the desired texture, soak beans before adding them to the cooker and add sugar and acid only after beans have cooked until tender.

• Dairy products and seafood tend to break down if they cook for extended periods. Unless otherwise instructed, add milk, cream, and sour cream during the last 15 minutes of cooking; add seafood within the last hour.

• The more "marbling," or fat, a cut of meat has, the more liquid it releases during cooking, requiring less liquid to be added.

• Fresh herbs and spices are better than dried for extended slow cooking times because they take longer to release their flavors. When using dried herbs, we recommend whole or crushed—not ground.

about cleanup

• Always allow the slow-cooker insert to cool completely before washing it. Cold water poured over a hot insert can cause cracking.

• Never immerse a slow cooker with a non-removable insert in water. Simply unplug it, and wipe clean with a cloth.

• We recommend using heavy-duty plastic liners for the easiest cleanup. If you don't use liners, be sure to coat the inside of the crock with cooking spray before adding contents.

• When using heavy-duty plastic liners, let the cooker cool, and then just toss the liner along with the mess.

top 10 slow-cooker tips

1. Resist the urge to lift the lid and peek at the slow cooker's contents, because it releases a great deal of heat. Each time you remove the lid when not required, you'll need to increase the cook time by 20 to 30 minutes.

2. Slow-cooker cleanup is a snap when using heavy-duty plastic liners made to fit 3- to 6½-quart oval and round slow cookers. Just fit the plastic liner inside your slow cooker before adding the ingredients. Once the meal is over and the cooker has cooled, just toss the plastic liner into the trash, leaving a crock that will require very little cleaning.

3. There's no need to stir ingredients unless a recipe specifically calls for it. And always layer ingredients as the recipe directs.

4. When making roasts or stews, pour liquids over meats and use only the liquids specified in the recipe. While amounts may sometimes seem low, more juices cook out and there's less evaporation than in conventional cooking methods.

5. Use silicon or plastic spoons, spatulas, and whisks to assemble and stir the contents of the slow cooker. They won't scratch the interior of the crock.

6. Newer slow cookers cook noticeably hotter than some of the original models. Be sure to double-check cook times depending on the age of your cooker.

7. To avoid soggy toppings, as well as to keep slow cooker juices from becoming watered down from condensation dripping into the crock, tilt the lid away from the food when removing it.

8. Remember that 1 hour on high equals approximately 2 hours on low. A bonus to cooking on low is that many recipes can cook a little longer than the recipe states without becoming overdone. Avoid cooking recipes with more fragile ingredients, such as dairy products, seafood, or rice, longer than specified.

9. Stews and casseroles cooked in the slow cooker tend to be forgiving in how long you cook them, so if you run a little late getting home, you're probably safe.

10. Before slow cooking, trim excess fat from meats. If you'd like, brown meat in a skillet or a broiler to remove fat and then drain the fat before adding to the slow cooker. When meats are done, use a gravy separator to quickly discard fat from pan juices. If time permits, refrigerate meats overnight to allow fat to rise to the surface and solidify; then easily skim the fat from the surface with a serving spoon and discard.

page 33

page 21

page 35

page 18

five-ingredient recipes

ready when you are

Whether you're looking for a recipe that slow-cooks while you run a few errands, go to work or play all day, you'll find plenty of options here that are easy to assemble and certain to satisfy just when you arrive home. They are arranged by the time they take to cook so you can easily pick a recipe that fits your schedule.

Quick and Easy
Mushroom Brisket

slow cooking over 8 hours

Quick and Easy Mushroom Brisket

makes 8 to 10 servings
ideal slow cooker: 4-quart

....

4- to 5-lb. beef brisket, cut in half
1-oz. envelope dry onion soup mix
8-oz. pkg. fresh mushrooms
¼ cup water

1. Place brisket, fat side up, in slow cooker.
2. In a mixing bowl, combine dry onion soup mix with mushrooms and water. Spread onion soup mixture over top of brisket.
3. Cover and cook on high 1 hour and then on low 8 to 12 hours.
4. Remove brisket from slow cooker and allow to rest for 10 minutes. Cut across the grain into thin slices. Serve with juices poured over top of sliced meat.

menu idea:

• Serve Quick and Easy Mushroom Brisket with buttered new potatoes and broiled tomatoes for an easy weeknight meal.

Italian Roast Beef

makes 6 to 8 servings
ideal slow cooker: 4- or 5-quart

....

2 onions, divided
2 garlic cloves
1 celery rib
3 slices bacon
All-purpose flour
4-lb. beef rump roast, cut in half
2 Tbsp. vegetable oil

1. Finely chop 1 onion, garlic, celery, and bacon. Mix together.
2. Lightly flour roast. Rub onion mixture on all sides. Cook roast in hot oil in a large skillet over medium-high heat until browned on all sides.
3. Slice remaining onion and place in slow cooker. Place roast on top of sliced onion.
4. Cover and cook on low 10 to 12 hours.

entertaining
Mexican Pot Roast

makes 8 servings
ideal slow cooker: 5-quart

....

1½ cups chunky salsa
6-oz. can tomato paste
1.25-oz. envelope dry taco seasoning mix
1 cup water
3-lb. beef chuck roast
2 Tbsp. vegetable oil
½ cup chopped fresh cilantro

1. In a mixing bowl, combine first 4 ingredients.
2. Cook roast in hot oil in a large skillet over medium-high heat until browned on all sides. Place roast in slow cooker and top with salsa mixture.
3. Cover and cook on low 8 to 10 hours.
4. Remove roast to a platter. Stir cilantro into sauce before serving with beef.

Pot Roast with Carrots and Potatoes

makes 6 servings
ideal slow cooker: 5- or 6-quart

3 to 4 potatoes, peeled and thinly sliced
3 to 4 carrots, peeled and thinly sliced
1 onion, chopped
Salt and pepper to taste
3-lb. beef brisket or beef rump roast
2 Tbsp. vegetable oil
1 cup beef consommé

1. Arrange potatoes, carrots, and onion in slow cooker.
2. Sprinkle salt and pepper over roast. Cook roast in hot oil in a large skillet over medium-high heat until browned on all sides.
3. Place roast in slow cooker over vegetables. Pour consommé around meat.
4. Cover and cook on low 10 to 12 hours.

variation:

: • Use a 10¾-oz. can cream of chicken soup and 1 cup strong coffee in place of beef consommé.

Barbecued Beans and Beef

makes 6 servings
ideal slow cooker: 3½- or 4-quart

1½-lb. boneless beef chuck roast
2 Tbsp. vegetable oil
1 medium onion, chopped
3 slices bacon, coarsely chopped
½ cup barbecue sauce
3 16-oz. cans baked beans

1. Cook roast in hot oil in a large skillet over medium-high heat until browned on all sides. Mix together onion and bacon in slow cooker. Top with roast. Pour barbecue sauce over roast.
2. Cover and cook on low 8 to 10 hours.
3. Remove roast from slow cooker and cut into ½-inch pieces.
4. Pour juices from slow cooker through a strainer into a small bowl. Reserve onion, bacon, and ½ cup of cooking juices. Discard remaining juice.
5. Return beef, onions, bacon, and reserved ½ cup cooking juices to slow cooker. Stir in baked beans.
6. Cover and cook on high 30 to 40 minutes more or until thoroughly heated.

note:

: • Select canned baked beans that are precooked with brown sugar and bacon. Do not use pork and beans.

15-minute prep

Zippy Beef Roast

makes 6 to 8 servings
ideal slow cooker: 4- or 5-quart

3- to 4-lb. beef roast, cut in half
2 Tbsp. vegetable oil
12-oz. can cola
10¾-oz. can cream of mushroom soup
1-oz. envelope dry onion soup mix

1. Cook roast in hot oil in a large skillet over medium-high heat until browned on all sides. Place roast in slow cooker.
2. In a small bowl, combine cola and mushroom soup. Pour over roast. Sprinkle roast with dry onion soup mix.
3. Cover and cook on low 10 hours.

variation:

: • Use a 10¾-oz. can golden mushroom soup and 1 cup cooking sherry in place of 10¾-oz. can cream of mushroom soup and cola.

Beach Boy's Pot Roast

makes 6 to 8 servings
ideal slow cooker: 3- or 4-quart

3- to 4-lb. chuck or top round roast, cut in half
8 to 12 slivers of garlic
2 Tbsp. vegetable oil
32-oz. jar pepperoncini peppers, undrained and sliced
6 to 8 large hoagie rolls
12 to 16 slices of your favorite cheese

1. Cut slits into roast with a sharp knife and insert garlic slivers. Cook roast in hot oil in a large skillet over medium-high heat until browned on all sides.
2. Place beef in slow cooker. Spoon peppers and all of their juice over top of beef.
3. Cover and cook on low 8 to 12 hours.
4. Remove meat and peppers from slow cooker; shred using 2 forks.
5. Spread on hoagie rolls and top with cheese.

Beach Boy's Pot Roast

Tortilla Soup

make-ahead

Spicy French Dip Sandwiches

makes 10 to 12 servings
ideal slow cooker: 4-quart

3-lb. boneless beef roast
½ cup water
4-oz. can diced jalapeño peppers, drained
0.7-oz envelope dry Italian salad dressing mix
10 to 12 crusty sandwich rolls

1. Place beef in slow cooker.
2. Combine water, jalapeños, and salad dressing mix. Pour over beef.
3. Cover and cook on high 1 hour and then on low 9 to 10 hours.
4. Remove beef and shred using 2 forks. Return shredded beef back to juice in slow cooker. Serve on sandwich rolls.

entertaining • kid-friendly

Party Meatball Subs

makes 30 servings
ideal slow cooker: 8- or 10-quart

10-lb. bag prepared meatballs
10 large fresh mushrooms, sliced
2 26-oz. jars roasted garlic spaghetti sauce
30 hoagie rolls
1 lb. grated mozzarella cheese (optional)

1. Combine all ingredients except the hoagie rolls and cheese in slow cooker. Stir well to coat the meatballs with sauce.
2. Cover and cook on low 8 to 9 hours, stirring occasionally throughout cooking time to mix juices.

3. Serve in hoagie rolls and sprinkle mozzarella cheese over top of meatballs, if desired.

serving tip:

• Place slow cooker filled with these Italian-style meatballs on a buffet along with hoagie rolls and cheese and let guests serve themselves.

15-minute prep

Sausage and Sauerkraut Supper

makes 4 to 5 servings
ideal slow cooker: 4- or 5-quart

1 lb. smoked sausage links, cut into 2-inch pieces
32-oz. bag refrigerated sauerkraut, drained
½ onion, chopped
1 apple, cored and chopped
2 to 3 Tbsp. brown sugar
Water

1. Combine first 5 ingredients in slow cooker. Add enough water to cover half the contents.
2. Cover and cook on low 8 to 9 hours.

Italian Sausage Dinner

makes 6 servings
ideal slow cooker: 4-quart

1½ lbs. Italian sausage, cut in ¾-inch slices
2 Tbsp. A-1 steak sauce
28-oz. can diced Italian-style tomatoes
2 green bell peppers, chopped
½ tsp. red pepper flakes (optional)
2 cups uncooked minute rice

1. Cook sausage in a large skillet over medium-high heat until browned. Drain well.
2. Place browned sausage and remaining ingredients except rice in slow cooker.
3. Cover and cook on low 8 hours.
4. Stir in uncooked rice. Cover and cook 20 minutes more.

healthy for you

Tortilla Soup

makes 6 servings
ideal slow cooker: 4-quart

4 bone-in chicken breast halves
2 14½-oz. cans chicken broth
2 14½-oz. cans stewed tomatoes
1 cup salsa
1 Tbsp. ground cumin
½ cup chopped fresh cilantro (optional)
Diced avocado (optional)
Baked Tortilla chips (optional)

1. Cook, debone, and shred chicken.
2. Combine chicken and remaining ingredients except cilantro, avocado, and chips in slow cooker.
3. Cover and cook on low 8 to 10 hours.
4. Stir in cilantro. Sprinkle with avocado and serve with chips, if desired.

tip:

• To save time, skip Step 1 and shred the meat from a grocery rotisserie chicken.

Beef Barley Soup

makes 8 to 10 servings
ideal slow cooker: 6-quart
pictured on page 10

3- to 4-lb. beef chuck roast, cut
    into 4-inch pieces
2 Tbsp. vegetable oil
2 cups coarsely chopped carrots
6 cups vegetable or tomato juice
1½ cups quick-cook barley

1. Cook roast in hot oil in a large skillet over medium-high heat until browned on all sides. Place roast, carrots, and vegetable juice in slow cooker.
2. Cover and cook on low 8 to 10 hours.
3. Remove beef and shred using 2 forks. Return shredded beef to slow cooker. Stir in barley and turn slow cooker to high. Cover and cook 30 minutes more or until barley is tender.

make-ahead
Bean and Bacon Soup

makes 6 servings
ideal slow cooker: 4-quart

1¼ cups dried bean soup mix
Water
1 onion, chopped
4 slices bacon, cooked and
    crumbled
1.25-oz. envelope dry taco
    seasoning mix
2 14-oz. cans diced tomatoes,
    undrained

1. Sort and wash beans; place beans in a large bowl. Cover with water 2 inches above beans; let soak overnight.
2. Drain beans, discarding water. Place beans in slow cooker and add 8 cups water, onion, bacon, and taco seasoning mix. Cover and cook on low 8 to 10 hours.
3. Stir in tomatoes. Cover and cook 30 minutes more.

tip:
• If you prefer a thick bean soup, mash some of the beans with a potato masher before adding tomatoes in Step 3.

Old-Fashioned Bean Soup

makes 8 to 10 servings
ideal slow cooker: 4- or 5-quart

1 lb. dried navy beans
Water
1 lb. meaty ham bones or ham
    pieces
½ cup chopped celery leaves
1 medium onion, chopped
1 bay leaf (optional)
1 tsp. salt
½ tsp. pepper

1. Sort and wash beans; place beans in a large bowl. Cover with water 2 inches above beans. Let soak overnight.
2. Drain beans, discarding water. Place beans in slow cooker and add 8 cups water, ham bones, celery leaves, onion, bay leaf, salt, and pepper. Cover and cook on low 10 to 12 hours.

15-minute prep
Potato Chowder

makes 12 servings
ideal slow cooker: 5-quart

8 cups peeled, diced potatoes
3 14½-oz. cans chicken broth
10¾-oz. can cream of chicken soup
¼ tsp. pepper
8-oz. pkg. cream cheese, cubed

1. Combine potatoes, chicken broth, chicken soup, and pepper in slow cooker.
2. Cover and cook on low 8 to 10 hours or until potatoes are tender.
3. Add cream cheese, stirring well. Cover and cook 20 minutes more or until cheese is melted.

note:
• Offer crumbled bacon, cheddar cheese, and chives as toppings for this hearty soup.

15-minute prep • kid-friendly
Rice 'n' Beans 'n' Salsa

makes 6 to 8 servings
ideal slow cooker: 3- or 5-quart

2 16-oz. cans black or navy beans,
    rinsed and drained
14-oz. can chicken broth
1 cup uncooked long-grain white
    or brown rice
1 qt. salsa
1 cup water
½ tsp. garlic powder

1. Combine all ingredients in slow cooker. Stir well.
2. Cover and cook on low 8 to 10 hours or on high 4 hours.

Caramelized Onions

makes 6 to 8 servings
ideal slow cooker: 4- or 6-quart

4 to 6 large sweet onions
½ cup melted butter or olive oil

1. Peel onions and slice off top and bottom ends. Place onions in slow cooker. Pour butter or olive oil over onions.
2. Cover and cook on low 10 to 12 hours.

note:

• Use Caramelized Onions as a filling for omelets or sandwiches, as an ingredient in soup, or as a side dish with grilled beef, pork, or chicken.

15-minute prep

New Year's Sauerkraut

makes 4 to 6 servings
ideal slow cooker: 3-quart

3 cups sauerkraut, rinsed and
   drained
½ to ¾ cup brown sugar
1 apple, cored and chopped
1 small onion, chopped
Water

1. Place sauerkraut in slow cooker. Stir in sugar, apple, and onion.
2. Add just enough water to cover sauerkraut mixture.
3. Cover and cook on low 8 to 9 hours.

The Simplest "Baked" Potato

15-minute prep

The Simplest "Baked" Potatoes

makes 4 to 6 servings
ideal slow cooker: 4- or 6-quart

4 to 6 large baking potatoes
Olive or vegetable oil
2 Tbsp. seasoned salt or your
   choice of dry seasonings
Toppings: butter, sour cream,
   crumbled bacon, shredded
   cheddar cheese, sliced green
   onions, sliced jalapeño peppers

1. Wash and scrub potatoes. Rub each unpeeled potato with oil.

2. Place seasoned salt in a zip-top plastic bag. Add potatoes, one at a time, and shake to coat. Wrap each potato in aluminum foil, and place in slow cooker.
3. Cover and cook on low 8 to 9 hours or until potatoes are tender.
4. Serve potatoes with desired toppings.

note:

• Slow cookers don't heat up your kitchen, even when it's hot outside. So turn on your slow cooker before heading out to the pool, beach, or garden.

Fajita Steak

up to 8 hours

editor's favorite • entertaining

Fajita Steak

makes 6 servings
ideal slow cooker: 4-quart

2 cups mild, medium, or hot salsa
8-oz. can tomato sauce
2 lbs. round steak, cut into 2-inch x
    4-inch strips
1.12-oz. envelope dry fajita spice mix
½ cup water (optional)
Flour tortillas
Accompaniments: shredded cheese,
    guacamole, sautéed red bell
    peppers

1. Combine all ingredients except flour tortillas and accompaniments in slow cooker.
2. Cover and cook on high 1 hour and then on low 7 hours more.
3. Serve on flour tortillas with accompaniments.

Sweet 'n' Sour Roast

makes 5 servings
ideal slow cooker: 2-quart

2-lb. beef roast
2 Tbsp. vegetable oil
½ cup pickle juice or apple cider
    vinegar
3 Tbsp. brown sugar
2 tsp. salt
1 Tbsp. Worcestershire sauce
1 cup water

1. Cook roast in hot oil in a large skillet over medium-high heat until browned on all sides. Place roast in slow cooker.
2. In a bowl, combine remaining ingredients. Pour over the roast.
3. Cover and cook on low 6 to 8 hours.

variation:

• Cube 5 medium-size potatoes and place in slow cooker. Add enough water to barely cover the potatoes. Top with 1 qt. frozen green beans. Add roast and continue with Step 2.

15-minute prep • kid-friendly

Meaty Spanish Rice

makes 10 servings
ideal slow cooker: 4- or 5-quart

2 lbs. ground beef
1 medium onion, chopped
1 green bell pepper, chopped
44-oz. can stewed tomatoes, diced
    tomatoes, or spaghetti sauce
1 cup water
2½ tsp. chili powder
2 tsp. Worcestershire sauce
1 cup uncooked long-grain rice
1½ to 2 tsp. salt
½ tsp. pepper

1. Brown beef, onion, and bell pepper in a non-stick skillet. Drain well. Place mixture in slow cooker.
2. Add remaining ingredients to cooker, stirring well.
3. Cover and cook on low 6 to 8 hours.

Cranberry and Honey Pork Roast

Easy Crock Tacos

makes 4 to 6 servings
ideal slow cooker: 4-quart

1 lb. ground beef
1 large onion, chopped
2 15-oz. cans chili beans
15-oz. can Mexican-style corn
¾ cup water
½ tsp. garlic powder (optional)
Taco shells

1. Brown ground beef and chopped onion in a non-stick skillet. Drain well.
2. Combine beef mixture and remaining ingredients except taco shells in the slow cooker, blending well.
3. Cover and cook on low 6 to 8 hours. Serve in taco shells.

entertaining • for the holidays

Cranberry and Honey Pork Roast

makes 6 to 8 servings
ideal slow cooker: 5-quart

3-lb. boneless pork loin roast
Salt and pepper to taste
2 Tbsp. vegetable oil
1 cup coarsely chopped fresh
    cranberries
¼ cup honey
1 tsp. grated orange rind
½ tsp. ground nutmeg (optional)
½ tsp. ground cloves (optional)
Fresh rosemary sprigs (optional)

1. Sprinkle roast with salt and pepper. Cook roast in hot oil in a large skillet over medium-high heat until browned on all sides. Place in slow cooker.
2. Combine remaining ingredients except rosemary sprigs in a bowl. Pour over roast.

3. Cover and cook on low 6 to 8 hours. Garnish with rosemary, if desired.

tip:

• If fresh cranberries are not in season, substitute a 16-oz. can of whole-berry or jellied cranberry sauce.

Honey Barbecue Pork Chops

makes 8 servings
ideal slow cooker: 4-quart

8 ¾-inch thick pork chops, divided
1 large onion, sliced and divided
1 cup barbecue sauce
⅓ cup honey

1. Place 1 layer of pork chops in slow cooker.
2. Arrange half of sliced onion over chops.
3. Mix together barbecue sauce and honey in a small bowl. Spoon half of sauce over chops. Repeat layers.
4. Cover and cook on high 1 hour and then on low 7 hours more.

Country Pork and Squash

makes 6 servings
ideal slow cooker: 5-quart

6 boneless country-style pork ribs,
    trimmed of fat
2 Tbsp. vegetable oil
2 medium acorn squash
¾ cup brown sugar
2 Tbsp. orange juice
¾ tsp. browning and seasoning
    sauce (we used Kitchen
    Bouquet)

1. Cook ribs in hot oil in a large skillet over medium-high heat until browned on all sides. Place ribs in slow cooker.
2. Cut each squash in half. Remove seeds. Cut each squash half into 3 slices.
3. Place squash slices on top of ribs.
4. Combine remaining ingredients in a small bowl. Pour sugar mixture over ribs and squash.
5. Cover and cook on low 6 to 8 hours.

Sweet and Saucy Ribs

makes 4 servings
ideal slow cooker: 3- or 4-quart

2 lbs. baby back pork ribs
1 tsp. black pepper
2 Tbsp. vegetable oil
2½ cups barbecue sauce
8-oz. jar cherry jam or preserves
1 Tbsp. Dijon mustard
¼ tsp. salt

1. Trim excess fat from ribs. Rub pepper over ribs. Cut into 2-rib portions and cook in hot oil in a large skillet over medium-high heat until browned on all sides. Place ribs in slow cooker.
2. Combine barbecue sauce, jam, mustard, and salt in a small bowl. Pour over ribs, making sure that each piece gets a good amount of sauce.
3. Cover and cook on low 6 to 8 hours.

tip:

• Try this delicious recipe using apricot, plum, or grape jam or preserves.

Scalloped Potatoes
and Ham

Scalloped Potatoes and Ham

makes 4 to 6 servings
ideal slow cooker: 4- or 5-quart

2 to 3 lbs. potatoes, peeled and cut into ⅓-inch thick slices
1 lb. cooked ham, cubed
1 small onion, chopped
2 cups shredded cheddar cheese
10¾-oz. can cream of celery or mushroom soup

1. Spray the interior of slow cooker with cooking spray.
2. Layer one-third of the potatoes, ham, onion, and cheese into the slow cooker.
3. Repeat procedure twice.
4. Spread soup on top.
5. Cover and cook on low 6 to 7 hours.

Chicken with Vegetables

makes 4 servings
ideal slow cooker: 6-quart

4 bone-in chicken breast halves
1 small head cabbage, quartered
1-lb. pkg. baby carrots
2 14½-oz. cans Mexican-style stewed tomatoes

1. Place all ingredients in slow cooker in order listed.
2. Cover and cook on high 1 hour then on low 7 hours more.

Chicken Cordon Bleu

makes 4 servings
ideal slow cooker: 4- or 5-quart

4 boneless, skinless chicken breast halves
½ lb. thinly sliced ham
½ lb. baby Swiss cheese, sliced
10¾-oz. can cream of chicken soup
6-oz. pkg. stuffing mix

1. Layer first 4 ingredients in slow cooker in order listed.
2. Prepare stuffing mix according to package directions and spoon over ingredients in slow cooker.
3. Cover and cook on high 1 hour and then low 7 hours more.

Greek Chicken

makes 4 servings
ideal slow cooker: 2- or 3-quart

1 lb. boneless, skinless chicken thighs
2 Tbsp. vegetable oil
1 onion, chopped
1 tsp. lemon pepper
½ cup plain yogurt
½ tsp. dried oregano

1. Cook chicken in hot oil in a large skillet over medium-high heat until browned on all sides. Place chicken in slow cooker along with onion and lemon pepper. Cover and cook on low 6 to 8 hours.
2. Remove chicken and shred with 2 forks.
3. Return shredded chicken back to slow cooker and stir in yogurt and oregano.
4. Serve plain or as a filling for pita bread.

Toscano Soup

makes 4 to 6 servings
ideal slow cooker: 4-quart

2 medium russet potatoes
1 lb. spicy Italian sausage
5½ cups chicken stock
2 cups chopped kale
½ tsp. crushed red pepper flakes (optional)
½ cup whipping cream or evaporated milk

1. Cut potatoes into ½-inch cubes. Place in slow cooker.
2. Grill, broil, or brown sausage in a non-stick skillet. When cool enough to handle, cut into ½-inch thick slices.
3. Add sliced sausage to slow cooker. Stir in remaining ingredients except cream.
4. Cover and cook on low 6 to 8 hours.
5. Stir in cream or evaporated milk 15 to 20 minutes before serving and cook until soup is heated through.

tip:
• If you don't want the soup to be too spicy, use ½ lb. sweet sausage and ½ lb. spicy sausage.

Indonesian Turkey

entertaining

Indonesian Turkey

makes 4 servings
ideal slow cooker: 2- or 3½-quart

3 turkey breast tenderloins (about
   1½ to 2 lbs.)
1½ Tbsp. grated fresh ginger
1 Tbsp. sesame oil
3 Tbsp. soy sauce
⅓ cup peanut butter

1. Place turkey in slow cooker.
2. Sprinkle with ginger, sesame oil, and soy sauce.
3. Cover and cook on high 1 hour and then on low 7 hours more.

4. Remove turkey from slow cooker with a slotted spoon. Stir peanut butter into remaining juices. If sauce is thicker than you like, stir in ¼ to ⅓ cup water.
5. Spoon peanut butter sauce over turkey to serve.

menu tip:

• Serve Indonesian Turkey with couscous and red bell pepper strips.

15-minute prep

Creamy Corn and Turkey Soup

makes 5 to 6 servings
ideal slow cooker: 3-quart

2 cups shredded cooked turkey
1 cup milk
2 cups chicken broth
15-oz. can Mexican-style corn
4 ozs. cream cheese, cubed
1 red bell pepper, chopped
   (optional)

1. Place all ingredients in slow cooker.
2. Cover and cook on low 7 to 8 hours.

Artichokes with Butter and Lemon

makes 4 to 6 servings
ideal slow cooker: 4-quart

4 to 6 artichokes
½ tsp. salt
1 cup fresh lemon juice, divided
2 cups hot water
½ cup melted butter

1. Wash and trim artichokes. Cut off about 1 inch from top. Trim tips of leaves, if desired. Place artichokes upright in slow cooker.
2. Sprinkle each artichoke with salt and 2 Tbsp. lemon juice.
3. Pour 2 cups hot water around base of artichokes.
4. Cover and cook on low 6 to 8 hours.
5. Serve with melted butter and remaining lemon juice for dipping.

Butternut Squash Soup

makes 4 to 6 servings
ideal slow cooker: 4- or 5-quart

49.5-oz. can chicken broth
1 medium butternut squash, peeled and cubed
1 small onion, chopped
1 tsp. ground ginger
1 tsp. minced garlic (optional)
¼ tsp. freshly grated nutmeg (optional)
Sliced green onions (optional)

1. Place chicken broth and squash in slow cooker. Add remaining ingredients.
2. Cover and cook on low 6 to 8 hours. Garnish with sliced green onions, if desired.

tip:

• For a creamy version of Butternut Squash Soup, puree soup in batches in a blender until smooth.

15-minute prep

Apples and Pineapple Dessert

makes 5 to 6 servings
ideal slow cooker: 4- or 5-quart

5 to 6 baking apples, peeled and cored
2 to 4 Tbsp. dark brown sugar
1 to 2 tsp. ground cinnamon
½ cup canned crushed pineapple, drained
¼ cup chopped walnuts

1. Slice apples and place in slow cooker.
2. Mix together 2 Tbsp. sugar, 1 tsp. cinnamon, and pineapple. Taste and add more sugar and cinnamon if desired.
3. Spoon sugar-juice mixture over apple slices. Stir together well. Sprinkle with walnuts.
4. Cover and cook on low 7 to 8 hours or until the apples are done to your liking.

Butternut Squash Soup

Savory Pork Roast

up to 6 hours

Savory Pork Roast

makes 6 servings
ideal slow cooker: 4-quart oval

2-lb. boneless pork roast
2 Tbsp. vegetable oil
1 garlic clove, minced
1 medium onion, sliced
1 pt. sauerkraut
1 tsp. caraway seeds
2 Tbsp. cornstarch
2 Tbsp. water

1. Cook roast in hot oil in a large skillet over medium-high heat until browned on all sides. Place roast in slow cooker.
2. Add remaining ingredients except cornstarch and water in the order listed.
3. Cover and cook on low 4 to 6 hours.
4. Remove pork and sauerkraut with a slotted spoon to a serving platter. Combine cornstarch and water, stirring until blended. Add to slow cooker; cover and cook, stirring occasionally, 15 minutes more or until thickened. Serve gravy with roast and sauerkraut.

15-minute prep
Zesty Italian Beef

makes 6 servings
ideal slow cooker: 3½-quart

1-oz. envelope dry onion soup mix
1 tsp. dried basil
½ tsp. garlic powder
½ tsp. dried oregano
¼ tsp. paprika (optional)
½ tsp. red pepper (optional)
2 cups water
2-lb. beef rump roast

1. Combine soup mix and seasonings with 2 cups water in slow cooker. Add roast to slow cooker.
2. Cover and cook on high 4 to 6 hours or until meat is tender but not dry.
3. Allow meat to rest for 10 minutes before slicing. Top slices with cooking juices.

Pepper Steak

makes 4 servings
ideal slow cooker: 3½- or 4-quart

1-lb. round steak, cut into ¾- to 1-inch thick strips
2 Tbsp. vegetable oil
14½-oz. can Italian-style stewed tomatoes, undrained
1 tsp. Worcestershire sauce
2 yellow, 2 red, and 2 green bell peppers, sliced in strips
1 large onion, sliced

1. Cook steak in hot oil in a large skillet over medium-high heat until browned on all sides. Transfer meat to slow cooker.
2. Combine tomatoes and Worcestershire sauce in medium bowl. Spoon over meat and top with vegetables.
3. Cover and cook on low 5 to 6 hours.

Fruited Pork

makes 6 servings
ideal slow cooker: 3- or 4-quart

2-lb. boneless pork loin roast
½ tsp. salt
¼ tsp. pepper
1½ cups mixed dried fruit
½ cup apple juice

1. Place pork in slow cooker. Sprinkle with salt and pepper.
2. Top with fruit. Pour apple juice over top.
3. Cover and cook on high 1 hour then on low 5 hours more.

Apricot-Glazed Pork Roast

makes 10 to 12 servings
ideal slow cooker: 5- or 6-quart

10½-oz. can condensed chicken broth
18-oz. jar apricot preserves
1 large onion, chopped
2 Tbsp. Dijon mustard
3½- to 4-lb. boneless pork loin, cut in half
2 Tbsp. vegetable oil

1. Combine broth, preserves, onion, and mustard in a bowl.
2. Brown pork loin in hot oil in a large skillet over medium-high heat until browned on all sides. Place roast in slow cooker. Pour glaze over meat.
3. Cover and cook on low 4 to 6 hours.

Cranberry Pork Loin

makes 6 to 8 servings
ideal slow cooker: 5- or 6-quart

3-lb. boneless pork loin, cut in half
2 Tbsp. vegetable oil
16-oz. can jellied cranberry sauce
¼ cup sugar
½ cup cranberry juice
1 tsp. dry mustard
¼ tsp. ground cloves (optional)

1. Brown pork loin in hot oil in a large skillet over medium-high heat until browned on all sides. Place pork loin in slow cooker.
2. Combine remaining ingredients in a bowl. Pour sauce over pork.
3. Cover and cook on low 4 to 6 hours.

Peach-Glazed Country Ham

makes 12 servings
ideal slow cooker: 4-quart

3-lb. boneless cooked ham
½ to ¾ cup brown sugar
2 Tbsp. prepared mustard
¼ cup peach preserves

1. Place ham in slow cooker.
2. Combine remaining ingredients in a small bowl. Spread over ham.
3. Cover and cook on low 6 hours.

variation:

• Use apricot preserves instead of peach.

Ham and Hash Browns

makes 4 servings
ideal slow cooker: 4-quart

26-oz. pkg. frozen hash browns
2 cups cubed cooked ham
2-oz. jar diced pimientos, drained
10¾-oz. can cheddar cheese soup
¾ cup milk
¼ tsp. pepper (optional)
4 ozs. shredded cheddar cheese (optional)

1. Combine potatoes, ham, and pimientos in slow cooker.
2. Stir together soup, milk, and pepper, if desired, in a small bowl until smooth. Pour over potato mixture. Stir gently.
3. Cover and cook on low 5 to 6 hours. Top with shredded cheddar, if desired, and let stand 5 minutes before serving.

tip:

• This recipe is perfect for a weekend brunch or a casual weeknight meal. Serve with fresh grapefruit, hot biscuits, and coffee.

Ham and Hash Browns

Spanish Chicken

Honey Baked Chicken

makes 4 servings
ideal slow cooker: 5-quart

4 skinless, bone-in chicken breast
    halves
2 Tbsp. butter, melted
2 Tbsp. honey
2 tsp. prepared mustard
2 tsp. curry powder

1. Spray slow cooker with cooking spray and add chicken.
2. Combine butter, honey, mustard, and curry powder in a small bowl. Pour sauce over chicken.
3. Cover and cook on high 1 hour and then on low 5 hours more.

entertaining

Orange Garlic Chicken

makes 6 servings
ideal slow cooker: 4-quart

1½ tsp. dried thyme
6 garlic cloves, minced
6 skinless, bone-in chicken breast
    halves
2 Tbsp. vegetable oil
1 cup orange juice concentrate
2 Tbsp. balsamic vinegar

1. Rub thyme and garlic over chicken. Reserve any leftover thyme and garlic.
2. Cook chicken in hot oil in a large skillet over medium-high heat until browned on all sides. Place chicken in slow cooker.
3. Mix together orange juice concentrate and vinegar in a small bowl. Stir in reserved thyme and garlic. Spoon over chicken.
4. Cover and cook on low 5 to 6 hours.

editor's favorite

Chicken Cacciatore with Green Bell Peppers

makes 6 servings
ideal slow cooker: 5-quart

1 green bell pepper, chopped
1 onion, chopped
1 Tbsp. dried Italian seasoning
15½-oz. can diced tomatoes
6 boneless, skinless chicken breast
    halves

1. Combine green pepper, onion, Italian seasoning, and tomatoes in a small bowl. Place one-third of tomato mixture in bottom of slow cooker.
2. Arrange 3 chicken breasts over tomato mixture. Spoon one-third of tomato mixture over chicken.
3. Top with remaining 3 chicken breasts and tomato mixture.
4. Cover and cook on high 1 hour and then on low 5 hours more.

serving tip:

: • Top with grated mozzarella or Parmesan cheese.

Spanish Chicken

makes 4 to 6 servings
ideal slow cooker: 3- or 6-quart

8 skinless chicken thighs
2 Tbsp. vegetable oil
½ to 1 cup red wine vinegar
⅔ cup soy sauce
1 tsp. garlic powder
4 6-inch cinnamon sticks

1. Brown chicken in hot oil in a large skillet over medium-high heat until browned on all sides. Place in greased slow cooker.

2. Combine wine vinegar, soy sauce, and garlic powder in a bowl. Pour over chicken.
3. Break cinnamon sticks into several pieces and distribute among chicken thighs.
4. Cover and cook on low 5 to 6 hours.

serving idea:

: • Serve Spanish Chicken on a bed of yellow rice and green peas.

Extra Easy Chili

makes 4 to 6 servings
ideal slow cooker: 4-quart

1 lb. ground beef or turkey
1¾-oz. envelope dry chili seasoning
    mix
16-oz. can chili beans in sauce
2 28-oz. cans diced tomatoes with
    garlic and onion
Cooked rice
Shredded cheddar cheese
    (optional)
Chopped onion (optional)

1. Brown meat in a large skillet. Drain well. Combine browned meat, chili seasoning mix, chili beans, and tomatoes in slow cooker.
2. Cover and cook on high 4 to 6 hours. Stir once halfway through cooking time.
3. Serve over rice and top with shredded cheddar cheese and chopped onions, if desired.

Hearty Lentil and Sausage Stew

makes 6 servings
ideal slow cooker: 6-quart

2 cups dry lentils, washed and
   stones removed
14½-oz. can diced tomatoes
8 cups canned chicken broth or
   water
1 Tbsp. salt
½ to 1 lb. pork or beef smoked
   sausage, cut into 2-inch pieces

1. Place lentils, tomatoes, chicken broth, and salt in slow cooker. Stir to combine. Place sausage pieces on top.
2. Cover and cook on low 4 to 6 hours or until lentils are tender.

Crabmeat Soup

makes 8 servings
ideal slow cooker: 3½-quart

2 10¾-oz. cans cream of tomato
   soup
2 10½-oz. cans split pea soup
3 soup cans milk
1 cup heavy cream
1 to 2 6-oz. cans crabmeat, drained
¼ cup sherry (optional)

1. Pour soups into slow cooker. Add milk and stir to mix.
2. Cover and cook on low 4 hours.
3. Stir in cream, crabmeat, and sherry, if desired. Cover and cook 1 hour more.

Loaded Potato Soup

makes 8 servings
ideal slow cooker: 6-quart

4 lbs. new potatoes, peeled and
   cut into ¼-inch thick slices
1 small onion, chopped
2 14-oz. cans chicken broth
2 tsp. salt
½ tsp. pepper
1 pt. half-and-half
Toppings. shredded cheddar
   cheese, crumbled bacon, or
   green onion slices

1. Place sliced potatoes in lightly greased slow cooker; top with chopped onion.
2. Stir together chicken broth, salt, and pepper; pour over potatoes and onion. (Broth will not completely cover potatoes and onion.)
3. Cover and cook on high 4 to 5 hours or until potatoes are tender.
4. Mash mixture with a potato masher; stir in half-and-half. Cover and cook 20 minutes more or until mixture is thoroughly heated. Ladle into bowls and serve with toppings.

Cheesy Broccoli Soup

makes 4 servings
ideal slow cooker: 3-quart

1 lb. frozen chopped broccoli,
   thawed
1 lb. loaf process cheese spread,
   cubed (we used Velveeta)
10¾-oz. can cream of celery soup
14½-oz. can chicken or vegetable
   broth
Dash of pepper
Dash of salt

1. Combine all ingredients in slow cooker. Cover and cook on low 5 to 6 hours.

Rosemary New Potatoes

makes 4 to 5 servings
ideal slow cooker: 3- or 4-quart

1½ lbs. red new potatoes,
   unpeeled
1 Tbsp. olive oil
1 Tbsp. chopped fresh rosemary
1 tsp. garlic-and-pepper seasoning

1. If the potatoes are larger than golf balls, cut them in half or in quarters.
2. Combine potatoes and olive oil in a bowl or zip-top plastic bag, coating well.
3. Add rosemary and garlic-and-pepper seasoning. Toss again until the potatoes are well coated.
4. Place potatoes in slow cooker. Cover and cook on low 5 to 6 hours or until potatoes are tender.

Ranch Hash Browns

makes 5 to 6 servings
ideal slow cooker: 6-quart

30-oz. bag frozen hash browns,
   partially thawed
8-oz. pkg. cream cheese, softened
1-oz. envelope dry ranch-style
   salad dressing mix
10¾-oz. can cream of potato soup

1. Spray interior of slow cooker
with cooking spray.
2. Place potatoes in slow cooker.
Break up with a spoon if frozen
together.
3. Mix remaining ingredients in a
bowl. Stir gently into potatoes.
4. Cover and cook on low 4 to 6
hours or until potatoes are cooked
through. Stir carefully before
serving.

Red Cabbage

makes 8 servings
ideal slow cooker: 3-quart

8 cups shredded red cabbage
1 cup white sugar
1 cup white vinegar
1 apple, cored and chopped
1 tsp. salt
1 cup water

1. Combine all ingredients in slow
cooker. Cover and cook on low 5
to 6 hours.

serving tip:

: • This is a great side dish to serve
: with grilled pork chops.

Red Cabbage

Chocolate Soufflé Cake

makes 10 to 12 servings
ideal slow cooker: 3-quart
pictured on page 10

18.25-oz. pkg. chocolate cake mix
½ cup vegetable oil
2 cups sour cream
4 eggs, beaten
3.9-oz. box instant chocolate
   pudding mix
1 cup chocolate morsels (optional)
Strawberry ice cream or frozen
   yogurt (optional)
Fresh strawberries (optional)

1. Combine cake mix, oil, sour
cream, eggs, pudding mix, and,
if desired, chocolate morsels in a
large mixing bowl.
2. Spray interior of slow cooker
with cooking spray. Pour batter
into slow cooker.
3. Cover and cook on low 5 hours
or until a wooden pick inserted
in center comes out clean. (Do
not lift the lid until the end of the
cooking time.)
4. Serve warm from the slow
cooker with ice cream or frozen
yogurt. Garnish with strawberries,
if desired.

Crab Spread

up to 4 hours

15-minute prep
Crab Spread

makes 8 servings
ideal slow cooker: 1- or 3-quart

½ cup mayonnaise
8 oz. pkg. cream cheese, softened
2 Tbsp. apple juice
1 onion, minced
1 lb. lump crabmeat, cartilage and
    shell bits removed
Celery leaves (optional)

1. Mix together mayonnaise, cream cheese, and juice in medium bowl until blended.
2. Stir in onion, mixing well. Gently stir in crabmeat.
3. Place crabmeat mixture in slow cooker. Cover and cook on low 4 hours.
4. Turn heat to warm setting to serve. Serve with toasted baguette slices and fresh vegetables. Garnish with celery leaves, if desired.

No-Peeking Beef Tips

makes 4 servings
ideal slow cooker: 4-quart

2 lbs. stew meat, cut into bite-size
    pieces
2 Tbsp. vegetable oil
1.25-oz. envelope dry onion soup
    mix
12-oz. can lemon-lime soda
10¾-oz. can cream of mushroom
    soup or cream of chicken soup
Cooked rice or egg noodles

1. Cook meat in hot oil in a large skillet over medium-high heat until browned on all sides. Place meat in slow cooker. Sprinkle dry onion soup mix over meat.
2. Combine soda and cream of mushroom soup in a bowl. Pour over meat, being careful not to disturb the onion soup mix.
3. Cover and cook on high 4 hours. Serve over cooked rice or noodles.

variation:

• For a creamier version, replace soda with 1 cup sour cream.

kid-friendly
Halloween Hash

makes 4 servings
ideal slow cooker: 2-quart

1 lb. lean ground beef
½ cup onion, chopped
16-oz. can whole-kernel corn,
    drained
16-oz. can kidney beans, drained
16-oz. can diced tomatoes
½ cup shredded cheddar cheese
    (optional)
Cooked rice or egg noodles
    (optional)

1. Brown beef and onion in a non-stick skillet until no longer pink. Drain. Place mixture in slow cooker.
2. Layer all remaining ingredients over meat mixture except the rice or noodles and cheese.
3. Cover and cook on low 2 to 4 hours or until thoroughly heated.
4. Serve plain or over a bed of rice or noodles. Sprinkle each serving with cheese, if desired.

Slow-Cooker Pizza

makes 8 to 10 servings
ideal slow cooker: 4-quart

12-oz. bag Kluski or sturdy noodles
1½ lbs. ground beef
32-oz. jar spaghetti sauce, your
    choice of flavors
16 ozs. mozzarella cheese,
    shredded
8 ozs. pepperoni, thinly sliced

1. Cook noodles according to directions on package. Drain.
2. While noodles are cooking, brown ground beef in a non-stick skillet. Drain off drippings.
3. Meanwhile, grease interior of slow cooker. Pour in one-fourth of spaghetti sauce. Follow with one-half the noodles, and one-half the browned ground beef. Top with one-third of the shredded cheese. Follow with one-half the pepperoni.
4. Repeat the layers. Top with the remaining spaghetti sauce and cheese.
5. Cover and cook on low 3 hours or until heated through and cheese is melted.

variation:

: • Add sliced mushrooms, sliced
: onions, sliced black olives, and
: diced green bell peppers to 1 or
: more of the layers, if desired.

Pork and Sweet Potatoes

Pork and Sweet Potatoes

makes 4 servings
ideal slow cooker: 4-quart

4 pork loin chops
2 Tbsp. vegetable oil
Salt and pepper to taste
4 sweet potatoes, cut in large
    chunks
2 onions, quartered
½ cup apple cider
Chopped fresh parsley (optional)

1. Cook chops in hot oil in a large skillet over medium-high heat until browned on all sides. Place chops in slow cooker. Add salt and pepper.
2. Arrange sweet potatoes and onions over pork.
3. Pour apple cider over all.
4. Cover and cook on low 3½ to 4 hours or until meat and vegetables are tender. Garnish with parsley, if desired.

Spicy Pork Olé

makes 5 servings
ideal slow cooker: 4-quart

1½ lb. pork loin roast, cut into
    bite-size pieces
2 Tbsp. taco seasoning
2 cups mild salsa
⅓ cup peach jam
2 Tbsp. cornstarch
¼ cup water

1. Spray slow cooker with cooking
spray.
2. Place pork in slow cooker.
Sprinkle with taco seasoning and
stir to coat.
3. Add salsa and jam. Stir until
well blended.
4. Cover and cook on high 3 to
3½ hours or until meat is tender.
Remove meat to serving dish and
keep warm.
5. Blend cornstarch and water in
a bowl. Turn slow cooker to high
and stir in cornstarch mixture.
Continue cooking, stirring
occasionally, until sauce thickens.
Serve over or alongside pork.

15-minute prep
Stuffed Pork Chops
and Corn

makes 5 to 6 servings
ideal slow cooker: 4- or 5-quart

6-oz. pkg. stuffing mix for pork
5 to 6 boneless pork chops
14-oz. can whole-kernel corn
10¾-oz. can cream of mushroom
    soup

1. Prepare stuffing mix according
to package directions. Place pork
chops in slow cooker and spoon
prepared stuffing mix over chops.

2. Spoon corn over stuffing. Pour
soup over all without adding water
to dilute soup.
3. Cover and cook on high 3 to 4
hours.

15-minute prep
Lemon Dijon Fish

makes 4 servings
ideal slow cooker: 2-quart

1½ lbs. orange roughy fillets
2 Tbsp. Dijon mustard
3 Tbsp. butter, melted
1 tsp. Worcestershire sauce
1 Tbsp. lemon juice

1. Cut fillets to fit in slow cooker.
2. Combine remaining ingredients
in a bowl. Pour sauce over fish.
3. Cover and cook on high 1 hour
and then on low 2 hours or until
fish flakes easily but is not dry.

tip:

  • If you have to stack the fish,
  spoon a portion of the sauce
  between layers.

15-minute prep • kid-friendly
Chicken in
Piquant Sauce

makes 4 to 6 servings
ideal slow cooker: 3- or 4-quart

16-oz. jar Russian or creamy French
    salad dressing
12-oz. jar apricot preserves
1-oz. envelope dry onion
    soup mix
4 to 6 boneless, skinless chicken
    breast halves

1. Mix together the dressing,
preserves, and dry onion soup mix
in a bowl.

2. Place the chicken breasts in
slow cooker. Pour preserves
mixture over chicken.
3. Cover and cook on high 3 hours.

serving tip:

  • Top each serving with coarsely
  chopped cashews.

Rachel's Chicken
Casserole

makes 6 servings
ideal slow cooker: 5-quart

2 16-oz. cans sauerkraut, rinsed
    and drained
1 cup Russian salad dressing
6 boneless, skinless chicken breast
    halves
1 Tbsp. prepared mustard
6 slices Swiss cheese
Fresh parsley (optional)

1. Place one-half the sauerkraut in
slow cooker. Drizzle with one-
third dressing.
2. Top with 3 chicken breast
halves. Spread one-half mustard
over the chicken.
3. Top with remaining sauerkraut
and chicken breasts. Spread
remaining mustard over chicken.
Drizzle with one-third dressing.
(Save the remaining dressing for
serving.)
4. Cover and cook on high 1 hour
then on low 3 hours more.
5. To serve, place a breast half on
each of 6 plates. Divide sauerkraut
over chicken. Top each serving
with a slice of cheese and a drizzle
of remaining dressing. Garnish
with parsley, if desired.

Chicken Divan

Chicken Divan

makes 4 servings
ideal slow cooker: 3-quart

4 boneless, skinless chicken breast
    halves
4 cups broccoli florets
2 10¾-oz. cans cream of chicken
    soup
1 cup mayonnaise
½ to 1 tsp. curry powder
Hot cooked rice (optional)

1. Place chicken breasts in slow cooker. Top with broccoli.
2. Combine soup, mayonnaise, and curry powder together in a small bowl. Pour over chicken and broccoli.
3. Cover and cook on high 3 to 4 hours or until chicken is tender. Serve with rice, if desired.

cooking tip:

⋮ • If you prefer crisp-tender broc-
⋮ coli, stir the broccoli florets into
⋮ the slow cooker during the last
⋮ 30 minutes.

Chicken with Tropical Barbecue Sauce

makes 6 servings
ideal slow cooker: 4-quart

6 boneless, skinless chicken breast
    halves
¼ cup molasses
2 Tbsp. orange juice
2 Tbsp. cider vinegar
2 Tbsp. Worcestershire sauce
2 tsp. prepared mustard (optional)

1. Place chicken breasts in slow cooker. Combine molasses, orange juice, cider vinegar, Worcestershire sauce, and prepared mustard in a small bowl. Brush over chicken.
2. Cover and cook on high for 3 to 4 hours or until chicken is tender.

menu idea:

⋮ • Serve Chicken with Tropical
⋮ Barbecue Sauce with grilled red
⋮ bell pepper wedges, pineapple
⋮ rings, and yellow rice.

Green Enchiladas

makes 8 servings
ideal slow cooker: 3-quart

2 10-oz. cans green enchilada sauce
8 large corn tortillas
2 cups chopped cooked chicken
1½ cups shredded mozzarella
    cheese

1. Pour a little enchilada sauce into slow cooker.
2. Layer 1 tortilla, ¼ cup chicken, and ¼ cup sauce in slow cooker.
3. Repeat layers until all 3 ingredients are used completely. Sprinkle with mozzarella cheese.
4. Cover and cook on low 3 to 4 hours.

tip:

⋮ • Green enchilada sauce can be
⋮ found in the Mexican foods sec-
⋮ tion in most large grocery stores.

Macaroni and Cheese

makes 4 to 5 servings
ideal slow cooker: 3-quart

1 to 3 Tbsp. butter, melted
1½ cups uncooked macaroni
1 qt. milk
8 to 12 ozs. shredded sharp
    cheddar cheese
½ tsp. salt
¼ tsp. pepper

1. Stir all ingredients together in slow cooker.
2. Cover and cook on low 3 hours.

Creole Green Beans

makes 4 to 6 servings
ideal slow cooker: 2-quart

2 small onions, chopped
¼ cup butter
4 cups fresh or frozen green beans
½ cup salsa
2 to 3 Tbsp. brown sugar
½ tsp. garlic salt (optional)

1. Sauté onions in butter in a saucepan.
2. Combine onion mixture with remaining ingredients in slow cooker.
3. Cover and cook on low 3 to 4 hours.

Bonnie's Baked Beans

Bonnie's Baked Beans

makes 12 to 14 servings
ideal slow cooker: 4-quart

½ lb. bacon, cut into ½-inch pieces
2 28-oz. cans pork and beans, drained
2 medium onions, chopped
¾ cup brown sugar
1 cup ketchup
1 red, green, or yellow bell pepper, cut into rings

1. Brown bacon in skillet until crisp. Drain.
2. Crumble bacon and place in slow cooker along with beans, onions, brown sugar, and ketchup. Stir well and top with bell pepper rings.
3. Cover and cook on high 3 to 4 hours.

kid-friendly
Golden Carrots

makes 6 servings
ideal slow cooker: 2-quart

2-lb. pkg. baby carrots
½ cup golden raisins
½ cup butter, melted
⅓ cup honey
2 Tbsp. lemon juice
½ tsp. ground ginger (optional)

1. Combine all ingredients in slow cooker.
2. Cover and cook on low 3 to 4 hours or until carrots are crisp-tender.

entertaining
Company Corn

makes 8 to 10 servings
ideal slow cooker: 3- or 4-quart

2 20-oz. pkgs. frozen corn
2 to 4 Tbsp. sugar
½ tsp. salt
½ cup butter
8-oz. pkg. cream cheese

1. Place frozen corn in slow cooker. Stir in sugar and salt.
2. Cut butter and cream cheese into little pieces and place on top of corn.
3. Cover and cook on low 4 hours, stirring occasionally if you're at home and able to do so. Stir just before serving.

Lemon Red Potatoes

makes 6 servings
ideal slow cooker: 3- or 4-quart

10 to 12 small to medium-size red potatoes
¼ cup water
¼ cup butter, melted
1 Tbsp. lemon juice
3 Tbsp. chopped fresh or dried parsley
Salt and pepper to taste

1. Cut a strip of peel from around the middle of each potato using a potato peeler.
2. Place potatoes and water in slow cooker.
3. Cover and cook on high 2½ to 3 hours or until tender. Do not overcook.
4. Drain potatoes.
5. Combine butter, lemon juice, and parsley. Pour butter mixture over potatoes and toss to coat. Season with salt and pepper.

Slow-Cooked Cheesy Potatoes

makes 10 to 12 servings
ideal slow cooker: 5-quart

30-oz. pkg. frozen hash browns
2 10¾-oz. cans cheddar cheese soup
12-oz. can evaporated milk
3-oz. can French-fried onion rings
¾ tsp. salt
¼ tsp. pepper

1. Spray interior of slow cooker with cooking spray.
2. Combine potatoes, soup, milk, one-half of the onion rings, salt, and pepper in slow cooker.
3. Cover and cook on high 3 to 4 hours or until potatoes are heated through.
4. Sprinkle remaining onion rings over top before serving.

Ranch Potatoes

makes 6 servings
ideal slow cooker: 4-quart

2½ lbs. small red potatoes, quartered
1 cup sour cream
1-oz. envelope dry ranch-style salad dressing mix
10¾-oz. can cream of mushroom soup

1. Spray interior of slow cooker with cooking spray.
2. Place potatoes in slow cooker.
3. Combine remaining ingredients in a bowl. Spoon over potatoes and stir gently.
4. Cover and cook on high 3½ to 4 hours or until potatoes are tender. Stir carefully before serving.

Raisin Nut-Stuffed Apples

makes 6 servings
ideal slow cooker: 4-quart

6 medium-size baking apples, cored
2 Tbsp. butter or margarine, melted
¼ cup brown sugar
¾ cup raisins
3 Tbsp. chopped walnuts
½ cup water

1. Peel a strip around each apple about one-third of the way below the stem end to prevent splitting.
2. Mix butter and brown sugar in a small bowl. Stir in raisins and walnuts. Stuff butter mixture evenly into the cavity of each apple.
3. Place stuffed apples in slow cooker. Add water. Cover and cook on low 3 to 4 hours.

healthy for you

Rhubarb-Pineapple Compote

makes 4 to 6 servings
ideal slow cooker: 3½-quart

1 lb. rhubarb
2 cups fresh pineapple chunks
½ cup orange soda
1 Tbsp. sugar
Pound cake
Grated nutmeg (optional)

1. Wash rhubarb and cut in 1-inch pieces. Place rhubarb in slow cooker. Stir in pineapple.
2. Stir in orange soda and sugar.

3. Cover and cook on low 4 hours or until rhubarb is tender.
4. Serve warm or chilled over slices of pound cake. Sprinkle each serving with nutmeg, if desired.

entertaining

Chocolate Fondue

makes 2½ to 3 cups
ideal slow cooker: 2-quart

½ cup butter, melted
1½ cups sugar
¼ cup whipping cream
3 Tbsp. crème de cocoa, rum, or orange-flavored liqueur
6 1-oz. squares unsweetened chocolate, chopped

1. Combine butter and sugar in slow cooker; stir well.
2. Stir in whipping cream and liqueur.
3. Stir in chocolate.
4. Cover and cook on low 2½ hours or until chocolate melts.
5. Stir until smooth. Turn heat to warm setting and serve directly from slow cooker with angel food or pound cake pieces, marshmallows, apple slices, banana chunks, and strawberries.

tip:
• As long as an inch or more of the fondue remains in the cooker, you can keep the cooker turned on low for up to 6 hours. Stir occasionally.

entertaining

Best Bread Pudding

makes 8 to 10 servings
ideal slow cooker: 5-quart

1 cup brown sugar, divided
16-oz. loaf raisin-and-cinnamon-swirl bread, torn
4 eggs
1 qt. milk
2 Tbsp. butter, melted
1½ tsp. vanilla extract
Caramel sauce (optional)

1. Spray interior of slow cooker with cooking spray. Spread ¾ cup brown sugar in bottom of slow cooker. Add torn bread. (Do not stir sugar and bread together.)
2. Beat eggs until smooth in a large mixing bowl. Beat in milk, butter, vanilla extract, and remaining ¼ cup brown sugar. Pour over bread.
3. Cover and cook on high 3 hours or until pudding is set and no longer soupy. Do not stir.
4. Let pudding stand 15 minutes before serving. Serve with caramel sauce, if desired.

Best Bread Pudding

Pizza Fondue

up to 2 hours

Pizza Fondue

makes 4 to 6 servings
ideal slow cooker: 3-quart

1 lb. pasteurized prepared cheese
   product, cut in ½-inch cubes
   (we used Velveeta)
2 cups grated mozzarella cheese
14½-oz. can Italian-style stewed
   tomatoes, undrained
Loaf of Italian bread

1. Place cheese cubes, grated mozzarella cheese, and tomatoes in a lightly greased slow cooker.
2. Cover and cook on high 45 to 60 minutes or until cheese is melted.
3. Meanwhile, cut bread into 1-inch slices and toast until lightly browned. Cut slices into 1-inch cubes.
4. Turn heat to warm setting and serve with toasted bread cubes.

variation:

: • Add ¼ lb. thinly sliced pep-
: peroni along with cheese cubes
: in Step 1.

15-minute prep

Reuben Appetizers

makes 10 servings
ideal slow cooker: 2-quart

½ cup mayonnaise
2 cups shredded Swiss cheese
½ lb. thinly sliced corned beef, cut
   into small pieces
14-oz. can sauerkraut, drained

1. Combine all ingredients in slow cooker.
2. Cover and cook on high 1 to 2 hours or until cheese is melted and mixture is hot.
3. Turn heat to warm setting and spread on slices of rye bread.

tip:

: • The consistency is best with
: regular mayonnaise. Do not sub-
: stitute fat-free mayonnaise.

15-minute prep

Meaty Queso Dip

makes 15 appetizer servings
ideal slow cooker: 3- or 4-quart

1 lb. ground beef
1 lb. bulk hot Italian sausage
1 lb. jalapeño pasteurized prepared
   cheese product, cubed (we used
   Velveeta)
10¾-oz. can golden mushroom
   soup

1. Brown ground beef and sausage in a non-stick skillet. Drain well and place in slow cooker.
2. Add remaining ingredients to slow cooker. Mix well.
3. Cover and cook on high 30 to 60 minutes, stirring frequently until cheese is melted.
4. Turn heat to warm setting and serve with tortilla chips. Stir occasionally to prevent scorching.

Bacon Cheddar Dip

makes 15 servings
ideal slow cooker: 4-quart

2 8-oz. pkgs. cream cheese,
    softened
2 cups sour cream
1 lb. bacon, cooked and crumbled
4 cups shredded cheddar cheese,
    divided

1. In a mixing bowl, beat cream cheese and sour cream until smooth. Fold in bacon and 3 cups cheddar cheese.
2. Place mixture in slow cooker and sprinkle with remaining cheese.
3. Cover and cook on low 1½ to 2 hours or until heated through.
4. Turn heat to warm setting and serve with white corn chips.

variation:

: • For a fresh herb version, add 1
: to 2 Tbsp. of your favorite fresh
: herbs to the cream cheese mix-
: ture along with bacon in Step 1.

Curried Cheese Dip

makes 9 to 10 servings
ideal slow cooker: 1- or 2-quart

2 cups shredded cheddar cheese
8-oz. pkg. cream cheese, softened
½ cup milk
¼ cup chopped scallions
1½ tsp. curry powder

1. Mix ingredients together in slow cooker.
2. Cover and cook on high 45 minutes to 1 hour or until cheeses are melted and dip is heated through. Stir occasionally.

3. Turn heat to warm setting and serve with crackers or fresh vegetables.

tip:

: • As dips are being served from
: slow cooker, stir occasionally and
: scrape down sides of slow cooker
: with rubber spatula to prevent
: scorching.

Norwegian Meatballs

makes 10 to 12 servings
ideal slow cooker: 3-quart

2- to 2½-lb. pkg. frozen meatballs
2 to 3 10¾-oz. cans cream of
    mushroom soup
12-oz. can evaporated milk
1½ cups sour cream
1 cup beef broth
1 tsp. dill weed (optional)

1. Arrange frozen meatballs in a long, microwave-safe dish and microwave on high 4 minutes.
2. Meanwhile, combine all other ingredients in a large mixing bowl, stirring well.
3. Place meatballs in slow cooker. Cover with soup mixture.
4. Cover and cook on high 45 minutes. (Sauce should not boil.)

serving tip:

: • Serve these meatballs as an
: appetizer or as a main dish with
: mashed potatoes or noodles.

Hot Chicken Salad

makes 8 servings
ideal slow cooker: 2-quart

2 Tbsp. minced onion
⅔ cup mayonnaise
2 Tbsp. lemon juice
1½ cups chopped cooked chicken
½ cup slivered almonds or pecans,
    toasted

1. Mix together all ingredients in slow cooker.
2. Cover and cook on low 2 hours or until thoroughly heated.
3. Serve hot on lettuce leaves with tomato wedges and crackers.

15-minute prep
Italian Chicken Nuggets

makes 4 servings
ideal slow cooker: 2-quart

13½-oz. pkg. frozen cooked
    chicken nuggets
⅓ cup grated Parmesan cheese
28-oz. jar spaghetti sauce
4 ozs. shredded mozzarella cheese
1 tsp. Italian seasoning

1. Place frozen chicken nuggets in slow cooker. Sprinkle with Parmesan cheese.
2. Layer in spaghetti sauce, mozzarella cheese, and Italian seasoning.
3. Cover and cook on high 1 hour or until chicken is tender and mixture is thoroughly heated.

Chicken Broccoli Alfredo

makes 4 servings
ideal slow cooker: 3-quart

8-oz. pkg. uncooked linguine or spaghetti

1½ cups fresh or frozen broccoli florets

1 lb. boneless, skinless chicken breasts, cubed

2 Tbsp. olive oil

10¾-oz. can cream of mushroom soup

½ cup shredded mild cheddar cheese

1. Cook linguine according to package directions, adding broccoli during last minute of cooking time. Drain.

2. Brown chicken in hot oil in a skillet 2 to 4 minutes.

3. Combine chicken, pasta, broccoli, and remaining ingredients in slow cooker.

4. Cover and cook on low 1 to 2 hours or until heated through and cheese is melted.

15-minute prep

Mexican Hominy

makes 6 to 8 servings
ideal slow cooker: 3- or 4-quart

2 29-oz. cans hominy, drained

4-oz. can chopped green chilies

1 cup sour cream

8-oz. jar processed cheese spread (we used Cheese Whiz)

1. Combine all ingredients in slow cooker.

2. Cover and cook on low 1 hour or until thoroughly heated and cheese is melted.

---

editor's favorite • entertaining

Flavorful Fruited Rice

makes 4 servings
ideal slow cooker: 2-quart

⅓ cup chopped onion

6-oz. pkg. long-grain and wild rice

2 cups chicken broth

¼ cup dried cranberries

¼ cup chopped dried apricots

Chopped fresh Italian parsley (optional)

1. Spray small skillet with cooking spray. Add onion and cook over medium heat about 5 minutes or until onion begins to brown.

2. Place onion and remaining ingredients in slow cooker, including the seasoning packet in the rice package. Stir well to dissolve seasoning.

3. Cover and cook on high 2 hours. Fluff with fork before serving. Garnish with parsley, if desired.

variation:

• Just before serving, sprinkle with ½ cup toasted pecans or other nuts.

Wild Rice Casserole

makes 4 servings
ideal slow cooker: 4-quart

6-oz. pkg. long-grain and wild rice

10¾-oz. can cream of mushroom soup

¾ cup water

2 Tbsp. chopped onion

2 Tbsp. butter, melted

1 Tbsp. beef bouillon granules

Dash of Worcestershire sauce (optional)

---

1. Place all ingredients in slow cooker, including the seasoning packet in the rice package.

2. Cover and cook on high 2 hours. Fluff with fork before serving.

---

editor's favorite

Oyster Stew

makes 4 servings
ideal slow cooker: 3½- or 4-quart

1 pt. fresh oysters with juice

¼ cup butter

2 cups milk

2 cups half-and-half

Salt and pepper to taste

1. Heat oysters in their own juice in a large non-stick skillet over low heat until edges just begin to curl. (Do not boil.)

2. Place oysters and their juice in the slow cooker.

3. Add butter, milk, half-and-half, salt, and pepper.

4. Cover and cook on low 2 hours or until heated through.

---

kid-friendly

Broccoli Soup

makes 8 servings
ideal slow cooker: 3½- or 4-quart

1 lb. fresh broccoli, chopped

¼ cup water

2 12-oz. cans evaporated milk

2 10½-oz. cans cheddar cheese soup

2 10½-oz. cans cream of potato soup

1 to 2 cups cubed pasteurized prepared cheese product (we used Velveeta)

Chinese Chicken Soup

1. Place chopped broccoli in medium saucepan. Add water; cover and steam briefly. Remove from heat while broccoli is still a bit crunchy. Set aside.

2. Mix milk and soups together in slow cooker.

3. Add broccoli and cooking water to slow cooker. Cover and cook on high 1 hour or on low 1½ hours.

4. Add cubed cheese 20 minutes before soup is done. Stir before serving.

15-minute prep

Chinese Chicken Soup

makes 6 servings
ideal slow cooker: 4-quart

3 14½-oz. cans chicken broth

16-oz. pkg. frozen stir-fry vegetable blend

2 cups cubed cooked chicken

1 tsp. minced fresh gingerroot

1 tsp. soy sauce

Fried wonton strips (optional)

1. Mix all ingredients except wonton strips in slow cooker.

2. Cover and cook on high 1 to 2 hours, depending upon how crunchy or soft you like your vegetables. Serve with wonton strips, if desired.

page 58

page 91

page 84

page 71

slow-cooker cookbook

There's a little something for every craving in this collection of slow-cooked favorites. Find main-dish solutions for holidays, weeknight family meals, and entertaining guests. You can even enhance meals with sensational side dishes and delicious desserts, too—all created in your slow cooker!

page 64

Red Pepper and Feta Toasts

fuss-free party favorites

Red Pepper and Feta Toasts

makes 12 servings
ideal slow cooker: 3- or 4-quart

2 Tbsp. extra-virgin olive oil
4 large red bell peppers, cut in 1-inch squares
½ tsp. salt
2 dozen French bread baguette slices, toasted
4 ozs. feta cheese, crumbled
Extra-virgin olive oil
Thinly sliced fresh chives (optional)
Freshly ground black pepper (optional)

1. Pour 2 Tbsp. olive oil into slow cooker. Stir in peppers and salt.
2. Cover and cook on low 2 hours.
3. Spoon peppers onto bread slices and top with feta. Drizzle with olive oil and sprinkle with chives and pepper, if desired.

Reuben Appetizer

makes 12 servings
ideal slow cooker: 2-quart

6 Tbsp. mayonnaise
2 Tbsp. Thousand Island dressing
10 ozs. Swiss cheese, shredded
½ lb. chipped or thinly sliced corned beef, chopped
16-oz. can sauerkraut, drained and cut in small pieces
1 tsp. caraway seeds (optional)

1. Combine all ingredients in slow cooker.
2. Cover and cook on low 2 hours, stirring occasionally, until cheese is melted.
3. Serve warm on sliced party rye bread.

prep tip:

• Use kitchen shears to snip sauerkraut into bite-size pieces.

Hot Beef Dip

makes about 24 servings
ideal slow cooker: 2-quart

2 8-oz. pkgs. cream cheese, softened
8 ozs. mild cheddar cheese, shredded
1 green bell pepper, finely chopped
1 small onion, finely chopped
¼ lb. chipped dried beef, shredded

1. Combine cheeses. Stir in pepper, onion, and dried beef. Spoon mixture into slow cooker.
2. Cover and cook on low 2 to 3 hours.
3. Turn heat to warm setting and serve with crackers.

variation:

• For a spicier dip, substitute Monterey jack cheese with peppers in place of cheddar cheese.

Butterscotch Dip

makes 10 to 15 servings
ideal slow cooker: 1-quart

2 11-oz. pkgs. butterscotch morsels
5-oz. can evaporated milk
⅔ cup chopped pecans
1 Tbsp. rum extract (optional)

1. Combine butterscotch morsels
and milk in slow cooker.
2. Cover and cook on low 1 hour
or until morsels are softened. Stir
with a wire whisk until smooth.
3. Stir in pecans and extract, if
desired.
4. Serve warm with apple wedges,
pear wedges, and pretzels.

editor's favorite

Black-Eyed Pea Dip

makes 12 servings
ideal slow cooker: 1½-quart

8 ozs. pasteurized prepared cheese
    product, cubed (we used
    Velveeta)
15.8-oz. can black-eyed peas,
    drained
4-oz. can chopped green chilies
½ cup butter, melted
4 green onions, chopped
Sliced green onion tops (optional)

1. Combine cheese, peas, chilies,
butter, and onions in slow cooker.
2. Cover and cook on low 1 hour,
stirring occasionally, until cheese
is melted. Cook 1½ hours more.
3. Turn heat to warm setting to
serve. Top with green onions and
serve with corn chips.

Butterscotch Dip

healthy for you

Slow-Cooker Salsa

makes 8 servings
ideal slow cooker: 1- or 2-quart

10 plum tomatoes, cored
2 garlic cloves
1 medium onion, cut in wedges
2 to 3 jalapeño peppers
½ medium-size green bell pepper,
    chopped
¼ cup chopped fresh cilantro or
    parsley (optional)
½ tsp. salt
¼ tsp. black pepper

1. Cut a small slit in two tomatoes.
Insert a garlic clove in each slit.

Place in slow cooker along with
remaining tomatoes and onion.
2. Cut stems off jalapeño peppers.
Place in slow cooker. Add chopped
bell pepper. Cover and cook on
high 2½ to 3 hours. Cool.
3. Combine the tomato mixture,
cilantro, salt, and pepper in a
blender. Cover and process until
smooth. Store in refrigerator up to
2 weeks. Serve with tortilla chips.

tip:

• Remove the seeds from the
jalapeño peppers if you prefer a
mild salsa.

15-minute prep • make-ahead

Cajun Boiled Peanuts

makes 18 cups
ideal slow cooker: 5- or 6-quart

2 lbs. raw peanuts, unshelled
¾ cup salt
12 cups water
3-oz. pkg. boil-in-bag shrimp and
    crab boil
⅓ to ½ cup hot sauce

1. Combine all ingredients in slow cooker.
2. Cover and cook on high 18 hours or until peanuts are soft. Drain well. Store in zip-top plastic bags in the refrigerator up to 2 weeks.

make-ahead tip:

• Freeze Cajun Boiled Peanuts up to 2 months in airtight containers. Reheat in microwave just before serving.

entertaining

Chicken Wings with Spicy Chili Sauce

makes 6 to 8 appetizer servings
ideal slow cooker: 3-quart

2½ lbs. chicken wings (about 13
    wings)
¾ cup maple syrup
½ cup chili garlic sauce (we used
    Tuong Ot Toi)
1 small onion, diced
2 Tbsp. Dijon mustard
2 tsp. Worcestershire sauce
Celery sticks

1. Cut off wing tips and discard; cut wings in half at joint.
2. Combine syrup and next 4 ingredients in a small bowl; reserve ¾ cup marinade and refrigerate. Pour remaining marinade into a large zip-top plastic bag; add chicken and seal. Refrigerate 8 hours, turning bag occasionally.
3. Remove chicken from marinade; discard marinade. Place chicken, skin sides up, on a lightly greased rack in a broiler pan. Broil, 3 inches from heat, 8 minutes or until browned.
4. Place chicken in slow cooker. Cover and cook on low 4 hours. Serve with reserved ¾ cup marinade and celery sticks.

5 ingredients or less • entertaining

Herb-Stuffed Mushrooms with Goat Cheese and Sausage

makes 22 appetizer servings
ideal slow cooker: 6-quart oval

½ lb. hot ground pork sausage
2 tsp. prepared minced garlic
4-oz. pkg. goat cheese
¼ tsp. dried Italian seasoning
½ lb. fresh button mushrooms

1. Cook sausage and garlic in a large skillet over medium-high heat, stirring until the sausage crumbles and is no longer pink. Drain sausage mixture and return to skillet.
2. Reduce heat to medium; add cheese and Italian seasoning to sausage mixture, stirring until cheese is melted. Remove from heat; cool slightly.
3. Clean mushrooms with damp paper towels. Remove stems and reserve for another use.
4. Spoon sausage mixture evenly into mushroom caps. Place stuffed mushrooms in a single layer in slow cooker. Cover and cook on low 2 hours or until mushrooms are tender.

Wassail

makes 16 to 18 servings
ideal slow cooker: 6-quart

1 gallon apple cider
6-oz. container frozen orange juice
    concentrate
6-oz. container frozen lemonade
    concentrate
½ to 1 cup brown sugar
1 whole nutmeg, broken in half
1 Tbsp. whole cloves
1 Tbsp. whole allspice
Orange slices
Cinnamon sticks

1. Combine cider, orange juice concentrate, lemonade concentrate, and brown sugar in slow cooker. Mix well.
2. Place nutmeg, cloves, and allspice in cheesecloth bag or spice ball. Add to juices in slow cooker.
3. Cover and cook on low 2 to 8 hours.
4. Before serving, float orange slices and cinnamon sticks on top.

entertaining • for the holidays

Red Hot Apple Cider

makes 16 servings
ideal slow cooker: 5- or 6-quart

1 gallon apple cider or apple juice
1¼ cups cinnamon candy hearts
20 cinnamon sticks, divided

1. Combine apple cider, cinnamon candy hearts, and 4 cinnamon sticks in slow cooker.
2. Cover and cook on low 1½ to 2 hours.
3. Serve hot with a cinnamon stick in each cup.

Johnny Appleseed Tea

makes 8 to 9 cups
ideal slow cooker: 4-quart

2 qts. water, divided
6 tea bags of your favorite flavor
6 ozs. frozen apple juice concentrate
¼ cup plus 2 Tbsp. firmly packed
   brown sugar

1. Bring 1 qt. water to boil. Add tea bags. Remove from heat. Cover and steep 5 minutes. Pour tea into slow cooker.
2. Stir in remaining ingredients.
3. Cover and cook on low 2 hours or until hot. Uncover and continue to heat on low while serving from slow cooker.

Lime-Cranberry Punch

makes 10 to 12 servings
ideal slow cooker: 4-quart

8 cups cranberry juice cocktail
3 cups water
½ cup fresh lime juice
⅔ cup sugar
3 4-inch cinnamon sticks, broken
   in half
Orange slices (optional)

1. Place all ingredients except oranges slices in slow cooker. Stir until sugar dissolves.
2. Cover and simmer on low 3 to 4 hours or until very hot.
3. Remove cinnamon sticks with a slotted spoon and discard before serving.
4. Float an orange slice on each serving of hot punch, if desired.

tip:
: • Refrigerate any leftover punch and reheat it or enjoy it cold over crushed ice.

Italian Hot Chocolate

makes 4 to 6 small servings
ideal slow cooker: 1- or 2-quart

2 cups brewed strong coffee
½ cup instant hot chocolate mix
1 4-inch cinnamon stick, broken
   into large pieces
1 cup whipping cream
1 Tbsp. powdered sugar

1. Place coffee, hot chocolate mix, and cinnamon stick pieces in slow cooker. Stir well.
2. Cover and cook on high 1 to 2 hours or until very hot. Discard cinnamon stick pieces.
3. Immediately after you've turned on the cooker, place electric mixer beaters and mixer bowl in the fridge to chill (this makes the cream more likely to whip).
4. Just before serving, pour the whipping cream into the chilled electric mixer bowl. Beat cream on high speed until soft peaks form.
5. Fold sugar into whipped cream. Beat again on high speed until stiff peaks form.
6. Ladle hot chocolate into small cups. Top each with a dollop of whipped cream.

Party Mocha

makes 10 servings
ideal slow cooker: 3- or 4-quart

½ cup instant coffee granules
6 0.71-oz. envelopes instant
   cocoa mix
2 qts. hot water
2 cups milk
Whipped topping (optional)
10 4-inch cinnamon sticks or
   peppermint candy sticks
   (optional)

1. Combine first 4 ingredients in slow cooker. Stir well.
2. Cover and cook on high 3 hours.
3. Stir and turn heat to low while serving.
4. To serve, pour into cups. Top each serving with a dollop of whipped topping and add a cinnamon stick or peppermint stick, if desired.

Hot Mint Malts

makes 6 servings
ideal slow cooker: 2- or 3-quart

6 0.25-oz. chocolate-covered
   cream-filled mint patties (we
   used York Peppermint Patties)
5 cups milk
½ cup chocolate malted milk
   powder
1 tsp. vanilla extract
Whipped cream, crumbled
   peppermint candy
Peppermint candy sticks

1. Combine mint patties, milk, malted milk powder, and vanilla in slow cooker.
2. Cover and cook on low 2 to 3 hours. Stir occasionally to help melt the patties.
3. When the drink is thoroughly heated, beat with rotary beater until frothy.
4. Top each serving with whipped cream and crumbled peppermint candy. Serve with peppermint sticks.

Hot Mint Malts

Roast Beef with Ginger Ale

mouthwatering meats

kid-friendly
Roast Beef with Ginger Ale

makes 6 to 8 servings
ideal slow cooker: 3½- or 4-quart

3-lb. beef roast
½ cup all-purpose flour
2 Tbsp. vegetable oil
1-oz. envelope dry onion soup mix
1.61-oz. envelope dry brown
    gravy mix
2 cups ginger ale
Fresh thyme sprigs (optional)

1. Coat the roast with flour. Reserve any flour that doesn't stick to the roast. Cook roast in hot oil in a large skillet over medium-high heat until browned on all sides. Place roast in slow cooker.
2. Combine the dry soup mix, gravy mix, reserved flour, and ginger ale in a bowl. Mix well. Pour sauce over the roast.
3. Cover and cook on low 8 to 10 hours or until the roast is tender. Garnish with thyme, if desired.

Burgundy Roast

makes 6 to 8 servings
ideal slow cooker: 4-quart

4-lb. beef or venison roast, cut
    in half
2 Tbsp. vegetable oil
10¾-oz. can cream of mushroom
    soup
1 cup burgundy wine
1 large onion, finely chopped
4 medium potatoes, quartered
4 medium carrots, quartered
2 Tbsp. chopped fresh parsley

1. Cook roast in hot oil in a large skillet over medium-high heat until browned on all sides. Place meat in slow cooker.
2. Blend soup and wine together in a mixing bowl. Pour over meat. Top with onion, potatoes, carrots, and parsley.
3. Cover and cook on low 5 hours or until meat is tender.

5 ingredients or less
Green Chili Roast

makes 8 to 10 servings
ideal slow cooker: 4-quart

3- to 4-lb. beef roast, cut in half
1 tsp. seasoned meat tenderizer
    (optional)
2 Tbsp. vegetable oil
1 tsp. salt
3 to 4 fresh green chili peppers,
    seeded and chopped
1 Tbsp. Worcestershire sauce
½ tsp. black pepper

1. Sprinkle roast with meat tenderizer. Cook roast in hot oil in a large skillet over medium-high heat until browned on all sides. Place roast in slow cooker.
2. Pour in water until roast is half covered.
3. Top with remaining ingredients.
4. Cover and cook on low 8 hours.

substitution tip:

  • Use a 4-oz. can green chilies in place of fresh green chili peppers, if desired.

Apple Corned Beef and Cabbage

makes 6 to 8 servings
ideal slow cooker: 5-quart

3- to 4-lb. corned beef brisket, cut in 6 to 8 pieces

3 to 4 medium potatoes, cut in chunks

2 to 3 cups baby carrots

1 qt. apple juice

1 cup brown sugar

1 small head cabbage, cut in thin wedges

1. Place corned beef in slow cooker.

2. Place potatoes and carrots around and on top of meat.

3. Pour apple juice over meat and vegetables. Sprinkle with brown sugar.

4. Cover and cook on high 1 hour; reduce heat to low and cook 8 hours more. Add cabbage and cook 1 hour more or until meat and vegetables are tender.

Apple Corned Beef and Cabbage

15-minute prep • kid-friendly

Slow-Cooker Beef Stroganoff

makes 6 servings
ideal slow cooker: 3-quart

1 lb. lean round steak cubes

1-oz. envelope dry onion soup mix

10¾-oz. can cream of celery soup

10¾-oz. can cream of mushroom soup

½ cup sour cream

1. Place first 4 ingredients in slow cooker and mix together thoroughly.

2. Cover and cook on high 1 hour; reduce heat to low and cook 5 to 7 hours more, stirring occasionally if you're around the kitchen and able to do that.

3. Stir in sour cream. Cover and cook 15 minutes more or until hot and bubbly. Serve over cooked rice or noodles.

---

5 ingredients or less

Braised Short Ribs

makes 6 servings
ideal slow cooker: 4-quart

1 cup plus 1½ Tbsp. all-purpose flour, divided

1 tsp. salt

3 lbs. beef short ribs, cut in serving-size pieces

2 to 3 Tbsp. olive oil

2 medium onions, sliced

1½ cups water, divided

1. Combine 1 cup flour and salt in a shallow bowl. Roll short ribs in the seasoned flour. Discard remaining seasoned flour.

2. Brown ribs on all sides in hot oil in a large skillet. Rather than crowd the skillet, which prevents the meat from browning, do the browning in batches. As you finish browning, transfer pieces of meat to the slow cooker.

3. Add sliced onions and 1 cup water.

4. Cover and cook on high 4 to 6 hours or on low 8 to 10 hours.

5. Remove fully cooked ribs to a platter and keep warm. Place remaining 1½ Tbsp. flour in a jar with a tight-fitting lid. Add remaining ½ cup water. Cover with lid and shake together until lumps disappear.

6. Turn slow cooker to high so that broth begins to simmer. When broth begins bubbling, add flour mixture to broth in a thin stream, whisking constantly. Continue whisking until broth thickens. Serve with ribs.

Wild Rice Ground Beef Casserole

makes 6 servings
ideal slow cooker: 3-quart

1 lb. ground beef
1 medium onion, chopped
6.2-oz. pkg. long-grain and wild rice, uncooked
4-oz. can mushrooms, drained
2 10¾-oz. cans mushroom soup
½ cup water

1. Brown ground beef and onion in a skillet over medium-high heat, stirring until ground beef crumbles and is no longer pink. Drain.
2. Combine ground beef mixture with remaining ingredients including the rice seasoning packet in the slow cooker.
3. Cover and cook on high 3 hours or on low 5 to 6 hours or until rice is tender.

Tortilla Casserole

makes 4 servings
ideal slow cooker: 3-quart

4 to 6 white or whole wheat flour tortillas, divided
1 lb. ground beef
1.25-oz. envelope taco seasoning mix
16-oz. can fat-free refried beans
1½ cups shredded cheese, divided
3 to 4 Tbsp. sour cream (optional)

1. Spray inside of slow cooker with cooking spray. Tear 3 to 5 of the tortillas into pieces and line the sides and bottom of the slow cooker.
2. Brown the ground beef in a skillet over medium-high heat, stirring until ground beef crumbles and is no longer pink.

Drain. Return to skillet and stir in taco seasoning mix.
3. Layer refried beans, seasoned meat, 1 cup cheese, and sour cream, if desired, over tortilla pieces.
4. Place remaining tortilla pieces on top. Sprinkle with remaining cheese.
5. Cover and cook on low 3 to 4 hours.

Cheesy Cheddar Lasagna

makes 4 servings
ideal slow cooker: 3-quart

1 lb. ground beef
14-oz. jar spaghetti sauce
1 cup water
12-oz. box shells and cheese, divided (we used Kraft Shells and Cheese)
8 ozs. cottage cheese
½ cup shredded mozzarella cheese

1. Brown ground beef in a skillet over medium-high heat, stirring until ground beef crumbles and is no longer pink. Drain. Return beef to skillet and stir in spaghetti sauce and water.
2. Place half the meat mixture into the slow cooker. Top with half the uncooked macaroni and half the contents from the cheese sauce packet.
3. Spoon cottage cheese over top.
4. Add remaining meat, remaining macaroni, and remaining contents from cheese sauce packet.
5. Sprinkle with mozzarella cheese.
6. Cover and cook on high 3 to 4 hours or on low 6 to 8 hours until macaroni is tender.

Tamale Casserole

makes 6 to 8 servings
ideal slow cooker: 4-quart

2 lbs. frozen meatballs
28-oz. can chopped tomatoes
1 cup yellow cornmeal
14- to 16-oz. can cream-style corn
1 cup chopped stuffed green olives
½ tsp. chili powder (optional)

1. Microwave frozen meatballs at 30% power 4 minutes or until thawed. Place in slow cooker.
2. Combine remaining ingredients in a mixing bowl. Pour over meatballs and stir well.
3. Cover and cook on high 1 hour. Reduce heat to low and cook 4 to 6 hours more.

Pork Barbecue

makes 9 to 12 servings
ideal slow cooker: 4-quart

3- to 4-lb. pork roast, cut in half
3 Tbsp. vegetable oil
16-oz. bottle hickory-smoked barbecue sauce
1 large onion, chopped
⅛ to ¼ tsp. ground cloves
Sandwich buns

1. Cook roast in hot oil in a large skillet over medium-high heat until browned on all sides. Place meat in slow cooker.
2. Cover and cook on low 6 to 8 hours or until very tender. Drain well.
3. Remove roast to platter. Using 2 forks, shred the meat.
4. Return shredded meat to cooker. Stir in barbecue sauce, chopped onions, and cloves.
5. Cover and cook on low 2 hours more. Serve on sandwich buns.

Tex-Mex Shredded Pork Sandwiches

makes 6 to 8 servings
ideal slow cooker: 4- or 5-quart

3- to 4-lb. pork butt roast, cut in half
2 Tbsp. vegetable oil
1½ 1.25-oz. envelopes taco
    seasoning mix
3 to 5 garlic cloves, sliced
1 large onion, quartered
4-oz. can whole green chilies,
    drained
1 cup water
Accompaniments: sandwich buns or
    flour tortillas, shredded lettuce,
    sliced tomato, and sour cream

1. Cook roast in hot oil in a large skillet over medium-high heat until browned on all sides. Place roast in slow cooker.
2. Combine taco seasoning mix, garlic, onion, green chilies, and water in a bowl. Spoon over meat in slow cooker.
3. Cover and cook on high 4 to 6 hours or on low 8 to 10 hours until meat is tender but not dry.
4. Place pork on a platter and shred with 2 forks. Stir shredded meat back into sauce.
5. Serve on buns or tortillas with shredded lettuce, tomato, and sour cream.

Tex-Mex Shredded Pork Sandwiches

Tangy Pork Tenderloin

makes 6 servings
ideal slow cooker: 4- or 5-quart

2 1.25-lb. pork tenderloins
⅔ cup honey
½ cup Dijon mustard
½ tsp. chili powder
¼ tsp. salt
2 Tbsp. cornstarch
2 Tbsp. water

1. Place pork in glass or ceramic baking dish. Combine remaining ingredients except cornstarch and water and spoon over pork. Cover and marinate in refrigerator 3 to 4 hours.

2. Drain pork, reserving marinade. Place pork tenderloins in slow cooker and top with reserved marinade.
3. Cover and cook on high 1 hour. Reduce heat to low and cook 5 to 7 hours more.
4. Remove pork to a serving platter; cover and keep warm. Turn slow cooker to high. Blend together cornstarch and water in a small bowl. When the juices in slow cooker begin to simmer, stir in cornstarch mixture until blended. Continue simmering, stirring occasionally, until juices thicken, about 10 minutes. Serve with sliced pork.

Italian Country Pork

makes 4 servings
ideal slow cooker: 4-quart
pictured on cover

¼ cup all-purpose flour
1 tsp. salt
½ tsp. pepper
4 10-oz. bone-in center-cut pork
   chops
3 Tbsp. olive oil
1½ cups finely diced carrot
1 cup chopped celery
1 cup chopped onion
2 cloves garlic, minced
½ cup chicken broth or dry white
   wine
14.5-oz. can diced tomatoes with
   basil, garlic, and oregano,
   undrained
1 Tbsp. chopped fresh rosemary
½ tsp. salt
1 bay leaf
Fresh rosemary (optional)

1. Combine flour, 1 tsp. salt, and pepper; dredge chops in flour mixture.
2. Heat oil in a large skillet over medium-high heat. Add chops and cook 2 to 3 minutes on each side or until browned. Place chops in slow cooker.
3. Add carrot, celery, onion, and garlic to pan; sauté until tender. Add broth, scraping pan to loosen browned bits. Cook 1 minute. Pour vegetable mixture over chops in slow cooker. Stir in tomatoes, 1 Tbsp. chopped fresh rosemary, ½ tsp. salt, and bay leaf. Cover and cook on low 5 to 6 hours.
4. Discard bay leaf. Top each serving with fresh rosemary, if desired.

Tangy Pork Chops

makes 4 servings
ideal slow cooker: 3-quart

4 thick-cut pork loin chops
Seasoning salt and pepper to taste
1 cup grape jelly
12-oz. bottle chili sauce

1. Rub pork chops with seasoning salt and pepper on both sides. Place chops in slow cooker.
2. In a small bowl, combine jelly and chili sauce. Spoon sauce over chops.
3. Cover and cook on high 1 hour. Reduce heat to low and cook 3 to 4 hours more.

tip:

• If the chops need to be stacked in order to fit into your cooker, make sure to top each one with sauce.

Pork Chops and Stuffing with Curry

makes 3 to 4 servings
ideal slow cooker: 3- or 4-quart

16-oz. box stuffing mix
1 cup water
10¾-oz. can cream of mushroom
   soup
1 tsp. curry powder
3 to 4 thick-cut pork chops

1. Combine stuffing mix and water. Place half in bottom of slow cooker.
2. Combine soup and curry powder. Pour half over stuffing. Place pork chops on top.
3. Spread remaining stuffing over pork chops and top with remaining soup mixture.

4. Cover and cook on high 1 hour. Reduce heat to low and cook 5 to 6 hours more.

Spareribs

makes 6 servings
ideal slow cooker: 4- or 5-quart

3 lbs. country-style spareribs
2 Tbsp. olive oil
2 small onions, chopped
1 cup ketchup
2 tsp. Worcestershire sauce
1 cup water

1. Brown spareribs, in batches, in hot oil in a large skillet over medium-high heat until browned on all sides. As you finish browning, transfer ribs to slow cooker.
2. Combine onions, ketchup, Worcestershire sauce, and water in a small saucepan. Simmer, stirring occasionally, 20 minutes. Pour over ribs.
3. Cover and cook on low 7 to 8 hours or until meat is tender.
4. Place ribs on a serving platter. Brush sauce over ribs. Serve additional sauce in a bowl along with ribs.

Asian Barbecue Ribs

Asian Barbecue Ribs

makes 8 to 10 servings
ideal slow cooker: 5- or 6-quart

6 lbs. country-style pork ribs, cut in
    serving-size pieces
¼ cup teriyaki sauce
¼ cup cornstarch
27-oz. jar duck sauce
2 Tbsp. minced garlic (optional)
Sesame seeds (optional)
Green onion tops (optional)

1. Place ribs in slow cooker.
2. Stir together teriyaki sauce and
cornstarch in a large bowl. Blend
in duck sauce and garlic, if desired.
3. Pour the sauce over ribs, making sure that each layer is covered.
4. Cover and cook on high 1 hour.
Reduce heat to low and cook 3 to
4 hours more. Top with sesame
seeds and green onion tops, if
desired.

Apricot Glazed Ham

makes 4 servings
ideal slow cooker: 6-quart

4 large cooked ham slices or ham
    steaks
⅓ cup apricot jam
¾ to 1 cup honey
⅓ cup soy sauce
¼ tsp. ground nutmeg

1. Place ham in slow cooker.
2. Combine remaining ingredients
in a mixing bowl. Pour over ham.
3. Cover and cook on low 4 to
6 hours.

Apple Raisin Ham

makes 6 servings
ideal slow cooker: 4-quart

1½ lbs. fully cooked ham
21-oz. can apple pie filling
⅓ cup golden raisins
⅓ cup orange juice
¼ tsp. ground cinnamon
2 Tbsp. water

1. Cut ham into 6 equal slices.
2. In a mixing bowl, combine pie filling, raisins, orange juice, cinnamon, and water.
3. Place 1 slice of ham in slow cooker. Top with one-sixth of the apple mixture. Repeat layers until you have used all the ham and apple mixture.
4. Cover and cook on low 4 to 5 hours.

tip:
• This recipe is a great way to use ham left over from holiday meals.

Ham and Dumplings

makes 6 servings
ideal slow cooker: 5-quart

2½ lbs. fully cooked ham
8 cups water
3 cups biscuit and baking mix
1 cup milk

1. Place ham and water in slow cooker.
2. Cover and cook on high 5 to 6 hours.
3. In a bowl, combine baking mix and milk. Drop by spoonfuls into slow cooker.
4. Cover and cook on high 1 hour more.

Cheesy Potatoes and Ham

makes 4 to 6 servings
ideal slow cooker: 4-quart

6 cups peeled, sliced potatoes
2½ cups cooked ham, cubed
1½ cups shredded cheddar cheese
10¾-oz. can cream of mushroom soup
½ cup milk

1. Layer one-third of potatoes, ham, and cheese in slow cooker. Repeat 2 more times.
2. Combine soup and milk. Pour over ingredients in slow cooker.
3. Cover and cook on high 1 hour. Reduce heat to low and cook 6 to 8 hours more or just until potatoes are soft.

Sausage Comfort Casserole

makes 6 to 8 servings
ideal slow cooker: 4- or 5-quart

2 lbs. beer brats or spicy sausage
2 14-oz. cans chicken broth
3 lbs. potatoes, sliced ¼-inch thick
Salt and pepper to taste
2 large onions, thinly sliced
6 ozs. sharp cheddar cheese, shredded

1. Spray slow cooker with cooking spray.
2. Brown sausage in a skillet over medium-high heat until browned on all sides.
3. Pour 1 cup chicken broth into slow cooker.
4. Arrange one-third potatoes on bottom of slow cooker. Sprinkle with salt and pepper. Top with one-third of the onions, one-third of the sausage, and one-third of the cheese. Repeat procedure twice.
5. Pour the remaining chicken broth over top.
6. Cover and cook on high 4 hours or on low 8 hours until potatoes and onions are tender.

Easy Sausage Sandwiches

makes 8 servings
ideal slow cooker: 5-quart
pictured on page 4

16-oz. pkg. bun-length smoked sausage
Water
26-oz. jar spaghetti sauce
8 hot dog buns
Sautéed bell pepper and onion strips

1. Place sausage in slow cooker. Add 1 inch water.
2. Cover and cook on low 3 hours. Drain well.
3. Stir in spaghetti sauce. Cover and cook 30 to 60 minutes more until sauce is heated through.
4. Serve sausage and sauce on buns topped with peppers and onions.

Fish Feast

catch of the day

Fish Feast

makes 6 servings
ideal slow cooker: 6-quart oval

1 large onion, sliced
1 green bell pepper, cut in 1-inch
   pieces
1 Tbsp. olive oil
14-oz. can fire-roasted diced
   tomatoes
1 Tbsp. minced fresh garlic
¼ cup dry white wine or white grape
   juice
2 unpeeled zucchini, sliced
6 7- to 8-oz. grouper fillets
½ tsp. dried basil
½ tsp. dried oregano
¼ tsp. salt
¼ tsp. black pepper

1. Sauté onion and bell pepper in olive oil in a large skillet 6 minutes or until tender. Add tomatoes, garlic, and wine; simmer 1 minute. Stir in zucchini.
2. Rinse grouper and pat dry with paper towels. Sprinkle basil, oregano, salt, and pepper over fish.
3. Place 3 fish fillets in a slow cooker coated with cooking spray. Top with one-half of vegetable mixture. Repeat procedure with remaining fish fillets and vegetables.
4. Cover and cook on high 2 to 3 hours, being careful not to overcook the fish.

serving tip:
• Serve with crusty French bread to absorb every delicious drop.

Salmon Soufflé

makes 4 servings
ideal slow cooker: 2- or 3-quart

15-oz. can salmon, drained and
   flaked
2 eggs, beaten well
2 cups seasoned croutons
1 cup grated cheddar cheese
2 chicken bouillon cubes
1 cup boiling water
¼ tsp. dry mustard (optional)

1. Coat the inside of slow cooker with non-stick cooking spray.
2. Combine salmon, eggs, croutons, and cheese in slow cooker.
3. Dissolve bouillon cubes in boiling water in a small bowl. Stir in mustard, if desired. Pour over salmon mixture and stir gently to blend.
4. Cover and cook on high 2 to 3 hours or until mixture is set. Let stand 15 minutes before serving.

Simple Tuna Delight

makes 3 servings
ideal slow cooker: 2-quart

1¾ cups frozen vegetables
12-oz. can water-packed tuna,
   drained
10¾-oz. can cream of chicken or
   cream of celery soup

1. Combine all ingredients in slow cooker.
2. Cover and cook on high 1½ hours, stirring occasionally.
3. Serve over hot cooked rice or noodles.

Salmon with Creamy Herb Sauce

makes 4 servings
ideal slow cooker: 5-quart oval

¼ cup sliced shallots
2 lemons, sliced
10 black peppercorns
2 bay leaves
1 cup chicken broth
1 cup dry white wine or chicken broth
4 6-oz. skinless salmon fillets (about 1-inch thick)
½ tsp. garlic salt
¼ tsp. crushed red pepper
¼ cup reduced-fat mayonnaise
2 Tbsp. reduced-fat sour cream
1 Tbsp. chopped fresh parsley
½ Tbsp. chopped fresh dill
1 tsp. Dijon mustard
½ tsp. fresh lemon juice
⅛ tsp. freshly ground black pepper

1. Place first 4 ingredients in slow cooker; add chicken broth and wine.
2. Cover and cook on high 2 hours. Meanwhile, sprinkle salmon with garlic salt and red pepper; cover and chill.
3. Stir together mayonnaise and remaining 6 ingredients in a small bowl; cover and chill herb sauce.
4. Place salmon on top of shallots and lemon slices; cover and cook on high 30 to 45 minutes more or until done. Carefully transfer salmon to a serving platter, using a large spatula. Discard cooking liquid from slow cooker. Serve salmon with herb sauce.

Tuna Noodle Casserole

makes 8 servings
ideal slow cooker: 4- or 5-quart

2½ cups uncooked noodles
1 tsp. salt
½ cup finely chopped onion
6- or 12-oz. can water-packed or oil-packed tuna
10¾-oz. can cream of mushroom soup
Half a soup can of water
½ cup shredded Swiss or sharp cheddar cheese
1 cup frozen peas
¼ cup slivered almonds, toasted

1. Combine noodles, salt, onion, tuna, soup, water, and cheese in slow cooker.
2. Cover and cook on high 2 to 3 hours, stirring occasionally.
3. Reduce heat setting to low and stir in peas and almonds; cover and cook 20 minutes more.

Caribbean Fish Pot

makes 6 servings
ideal slow cooker: 4½-quart

2 tsp. oil
2 cups diced peeled red potato
1 cup chopped onion
¾ cup diced red bell pepper
⅔ cup chopped celery
4 garlic cloves, minced
2 14½-oz. cans diced tomatoes with garlic and onion, undrained
2 8-oz. bottles clam juice
3 Tbsp. pickled jalapeño pepper slices, minced
1 tsp. dried thyme
¼ tsp. ground allspice
¾-lb. grouper or other firm white fish fillet, cut into 1-inch cubes
¾ lb. unpeeled, large raw shrimp, peeled and deveined

1. Heat oil in a large non-stick skillet over medium-high heat. Add potato and next 3 ingredients; sauté 5 minutes. Add garlic; sauté 30 seconds. Cover, reduce heat to medium, and cook 5 minutes or until potato is tender.
2. Place potato mixture in slow cooker. Add tomatoes and next 4 ingredients; stir well. Cover and cook on low 7 hours. Stir in grouper and shrimp. Cover and cook 45 minutes more or until fish flakes easily when tested with a fork.

Cioppino

makes 6 servings
ideal slow cooker: 4½-quart

1 Tbsp. olive oil
2 cups chopped onion
1½ cups chopped celery
1½ cups diced green bell pepper
4 garlic cloves, minced
2 10-oz. cans diced tomatoes with green chiles, undrained
1 8-oz. bottle clam juice
1 6-oz. can tomato paste
1 cup dry white wine
3 Tbsp. red wine vinegar
1 tsp. dried thyme
¼ tsp. crushed red pepper
1¼ lbs. little neck clams (about 24), scrubbed
1 lb. unpeeled, large raw shrimp, peeled and deveined
½-lb. grouper or other firm white fish fillet, cut into 1-inch cubes
½-lb. lump crabmeat, drained and shell pieces removed
Fresh thyme sprigs (optional)

1. Heat oil in a large non-stick skillet over medium-high heat. Add onion and next 3 ingredients; sauté 6 minutes or until vegetables are tender.

2. Place onion mixture in slow cooker. Add tomatoes and next 6 ingredients; stir well. Cover and cook on low 6 hours.

3. Increase heat to high. Add clams; cover and cook 20 minutes more.

4. Add shrimp, grouper, and crabmeat; cover and cook 10 to 15 minutes or until clams open and fish flakes easily when tested with a fork. Discard any unopened shells. Garnish with thyme sprigs, if desired.

Company Seafood Pasta

makes 8 servings
ideal slow cooker: 4-quart

½ lb. bay scallops
1 to 2 Tbsp. butter or margarine, melted
2 cups sour cream
1¼ cups shredded Monterey jack cheese
½ lb. fresh crabmeat
⅛ tsp. pepper
1 lb. unpeeled, medium-size raw shrimp, cooked and peeled
4 cups cooked linguine
Chopped fresh parsley (optional)

1. Sear scallops 1 minute on each side in a large skillet in hot butter. Transfer scallops to slow cooker.

2. Combine sour cream and cheese; add to slow cooker along with crab, pepper, and shrimp. Stir gently to blend.

3. Cover and cook on low 1 to 2 hours.

4. Serve seafood mixture over linguine. Garnish with fresh parsley, if desired.

Rich and Easy Clam Chowder

makes 4 to 5 servings
ideal slow cooker: 4- or 5-quart

3 10¾-oz. cans cream of potato soup
2 10¾-oz. cans New England clam chowder
½ cup butter
1 small onion, diced
2 cups half-and-half
2 6½-oz. cans chopped clams, undrained
Freshly ground black pepper

1. Combine first 6 ingredients in slow cooker. Cover and cook on low 2 to 4 hours. Serve with freshly ground black pepper.

Shrimp Creole

makes 8 to 10 servings
ideal slow cooker: 4- or 5-quart

¼ cup canola oil
⅓ cup all-purpose flour
1¾ cups sliced onion
1 cup diced green bell pepper
1 cup diced celery
1½ large carrots, shredded
2¾-lb. can diced tomatoes
¾ cup water
½ tsp. dried thyme
1 garlic clove, minced
Pinch of dried rosemary
1 Tbsp. sugar
3 bay leaves
1 Tbsp. Worcestershire sauce
¾ tsp. salt
⅛ tsp. dried oregano
2½ lbs. unpeeled, large raw shrimp, peeled and deveined
Hot cooked rice

1. Combine canola oil and flour in a skillet. Cook, stirring constantly, over medium-high heat until

mixture is medium brown. Add onion, bell pepper, celery, and carrot. Cook 5 to 10 minutes. Transfer mixture to slow cooker.

2. Stir in remaining ingredients except shrimp and rice. Cover and cook on low 4 to 6 hours.

3. Stir in shrimp; cover and cook 1 hour more.

4. Remove and discard bay leaves. Serve Shrimp Creole over rice.

Thai Coconut Shrimp and Rice

makes 6 servings
ideal slow cooker: 5-quart
pictured on page 52

3 cups red bell pepper strips
2 cups chicken broth
1½ cups uncooked converted rice (we used Uncle Ben's)
½ cup thinly sliced carrot
1½ tsp. Thai chili garlic paste
2 8-oz bottles clam juice
1 14-oz. can coconut milk
10 ⅛-inch slices peeled fresh ginger
5 garlic cloves, minced
1½ lbs. unpeeled, large raw shrimp, peeled and deveined
2 cups fresh sugar snap peas, trimmed
½ cup sliced green onion tops
⅓ cup fresh lime juice
⅛ tsp. salt
¼ cup flaked sweetened coconut, toasted (optional)

1. Place first 9 ingredients in slow cooker; stir well. Cover and cook on low 4 hours.

2. Increase heat to high. Add shrimp and next 4 ingredients; cover and cook 30 minutes more or until shrimp are done. Spoon into bowls; sprinkle with coconut, if desired.

Tamale Chicken

pleasing poultry

Tamale Chicken

makes 6 servings
ideal slow cooker: 4-quart

1 medium onion, chopped
2 Tbsp. vegetable oil
16-oz. can beef tamales, drained
10¾-oz. can cream of chicken soup
1 cup sour cream
1 cup sliced ripe olives
1 cup chopped stewed tomatoes
2 cups shredded cheddar cheese
8 chicken breast halves, cooked and
    chopped
4-oz. can chopped green chilies
1 tsp. chili powder
1 tsp. garlic powder
1 tsp. pepper
1½ cups shredded cheddar cheese,
    divided
Chopped fresh tomato (optional)
Shredded lettuce (optional)
Sour cream (optional)
Prepared guacamole (optional)

1. Sauté onion in oil in large skillet.
2. Unwrap tamales and coarsely chop. Combine onion, chopped tamales, and next 10 ingredients. Pour into slow cooker. Top with ½ cup shredded cheddar cheese.
3. Cover and cook on high 3 to 4 hours.
4. Serve with remaining cheddar cheese and, if desired, tomato, lettuce, sour cream, and guacamole.

serving idea:

• Soak dried corn husks in warm water until softened. For each serving, layer about three corn husks one on top of the other and tie ends with extra strips of softened corn husks. Shape the stacked husks into an individual serving boat. Spoon Tamale Chicken mixture into boat to serve.

California Chicken

makes 4 to 6 servings
ideal slow cooker: 4-quart

3-lb. chicken, quartered, skin
    removed, trimmed of visible fat
1 cup orange juice
⅓ cup chili sauce
2 Tbsp. soy sauce
1 Tbsp. molasses
1 tsp. dry mustard
¼ tsp. garlic powder
¼ tsp. onion powder
2 Tbsp. chopped green bell pepper
3 medium oranges, peeled and
    separated into slices, or 13½-oz.
    can mandarin oranges, drained

1. Arrange chicken in slow cooker.
2. In separate bowl, combine orange juice, chili sauce, soy sauce, molasses, dry mustard, garlic powder, and onion powder. Pour over chicken.
3. Cover and cook on high 1 hour and then on low 7 to 8 hours.
4. Stir in green bell pepper and oranges. Cover and cook 30 minutes.

**Blue Ribbon
Cranberry Chicken**

5 ingredients or less

Blue Ribbon Cranberry Chicken

makes 4 to 6 servings
ideal slow cooker: 4- or 5-quart

2½- to 3-lb. chicken, cut up

16-oz. can whole-berry cranberry
  sauce

8-oz. bottle Russian salad
  dressing

1-oz. envelope dry onion soup
  mix

1. Rinse chicken and pat dry with paper towels. Place chicken in slow cooker.

2. Combine cranberry sauce, salad dressing, and soup mix. Pour over chicken.

3. Cover with slow cooker lid and chill 1 to 8 hours or overnight.

4. Without removing cover, cook on high 4 hours or on high 1 hour and then on low 5 to 7 hours. Serve chicken and sauce over noodles or rice.

15-minute prep

Cranberry Chicken Barbecue

makes 6 to 8 servings
ideal slow cooker: 4- or 5-quart

4 lbs. chicken pieces, divided

½ tsp. salt

¼ tsp. pepper

½ cup diced celery

½ cup diced onion

16-oz. can whole-berry cranberry
  sauce

1 cup barbecue sauce

1. Sprinkle chicken with salt and pepper. Place one-third of chicken pieces, celery, and onion in the slow cooker.

2. Combine cranberry sauce and barbecue sauce in a mixing bowl. Spoon one-third of the sauce over the chicken in the cooker.

3. Repeat procedure with chicken, celery, onion, and sauce twice.

4. Cover and cook on high 4 hours or on high 1 hour and then on low 5 to 7 hours.

---

5 ingredients or less

Spicy Chicken Curry

makes 10 servings
ideal slow cooker: 4- or 5-quart

. . . .

10 skinless chicken breast halves, divided
16-oz. jar mild, medium, or hot salsa
1 medium onion, chopped
2 Tbsp. curry powder
1 cup sour cream

1. Place half the chicken in the slow cooker.

2. Combine salsa, onion, and curry powder in a medium bowl. Pour half the sauce over the chicken in the cooker. Repeat layers.

3. Cover and cook on high 3 hours or on high 1½ hours and then on low 3 hours.

4. Remove chicken to serving platter and cover to keep warm.

5. Add sour cream to slow cooker and stir into salsa mixture until well blended. Serve over chicken.

15-minute prep

Chicken à la Orange

makes 8 servings
ideal slow cooker: 4-quart

. . . .

8 boneless, skinless chicken breast halves
½ cup chopped onion
12-oz. jar orange marmalade
½ cup Russian dressing
2 oranges, peeled and sliced
1 Tbsp. chopped fresh parsley

1. Place chicken and onion in slow cooker.

2. Combine marmalade and dressing. Pour over chicken.

3. Cover and cook on high 1 hour and then on low 3 to 5 hours.

4. Top with orange slices and sprinkle with parsley. Serve with rice.

Lemon Garlic Chicken

makes 4 servings
ideal slow cooker: 3½-quart

. . . .

1 tsp. dried oregano
½ tsp. seasoned salt
¼ tsp. black pepper
4 skinless chicken breast halves
2 Tbsp. butter or margarine
¼ cup water
3 Tbsp. lemon juice
2 garlic cloves, minced
1 tsp. chicken bouillon granules
1 tsp. minced fresh parsley

1. Combine oregano, salt, and pepper. Rub all of mixture into chicken. Brown chicken in butter or margarine in skillet. Transfer to slow cooker.

2. Add water, lemon juice, garlic, and bouillon granules to skillet. Bring to boil, loosening browned bits from skillet with a spatula. Pour over chicken.

---

3. Cover and cook on high 2½ hours or on high 1 hour and then on low 3 to 4 hours.

4. Add parsley and baste chicken. Cover and cook on high 15 to 30 minutes more or until chicken is tender.

Mushroom Chicken in Sour Cream Sauce

makes 6 servings
ideal slow cooker: 4-quart

. . . .

¼ tsp. salt
¼ tsp. pepper
½ tsp. paprika
¼ tsp. lemon pepper
1 tsp. garlic powder
6 skinless chicken breast halves
10¾-oz. can cream of mushroom soup
8-oz. container sour cream
½ cup dry white wine or chicken broth
½ lb. fresh mushrooms, sliced

1. Combine salt, pepper, paprika, lemon pepper, and garlic powder. Rub over chicken. Place in slow cooker.

2. Combine soup, sour cream, and wine. Stir in mushrooms. Pour over chicken.

3. Cover and cook on high 5 hours or on high 1 hour and then on low 5 to 7 hours.

menu tip:

: • Serve over potatoes, rice, or
: couscous. It is also delicious
: accompanied with a broccoli-
: cauliflower salad and applesauce.

Uncle Tim's Chicken and Sauerkraut

makes 4 servings
ideal slow cooker: 3½-quart

4 large boneless, skinless chicken
    breast halves
1-lb. bag sauerkraut
12-oz. can beer
8 medium-size red potatoes,
    washed and quartered
Salt and pepper to taste
Water

1. Place chicken in slow cooker.
Spoon sauerkraut over chicken.
2. Pour beer into slow cooker and
add potatoes. Sprinkle generously
with salt and pepper.
3. Pour water over all until
everything is just covered.
4. Cover and cook on high 5 hours
or on high 1 hour and then on
low 7 hours or until chicken and
potatoes are tender.

Szechwan-Style Chicken and Broccoli

makes 4 servings
ideal slow cooker: 4-quart

4 boneless, skinless chicken breast
    halves
1 Tbsp. canola oil
½ cup picante sauce
2 Tbsp. soy sauce
½ tsp. sugar
½ Tbsp. quick-cooking tapioca
1 medium onion, chopped
2 garlic cloves, minced
½ tsp. ground ginger
2 cups broccoli florets
1 medium-size red bell pepper, cut
    into pieces

1. Cut chicken into 1-inch cubes
and brown lightly in oil in skillet.

Place in slow cooker.
2. Stir in remaining ingredients.
3. Cover and cook on high 1 to
1½ hours or on high 1 hour and
then on low 1 to 2 hours.

entertaining

Bacon-Feta Stuffed Chicken

makes 4 servings
ideal slow cooker: 3-quart

¼ cup crumbled cooked bacon
¼ cup crumbled feta cheese
4 boneless, skinless chicken breast
    halves
2 14½-oz. cans diced tomatoes
1 Tbsp. dried basil

1. In a small bowl, mix bacon and
cheese together lightly.
2. Cut a pocket in the thicker side
of each chicken breast. Fill each
with one-fourth of the bacon and
cheese. Pinch shut and secure
with toothpicks.
3. Place chicken in slow cooker.
Top with tomatoes and sprinkle
with basil.
4. Cover and cook on high 1½
to 3 hours or until chicken is
tender.

Slow-Cooker Creamy Chicken Italian

makes 6 servings
ideal slow cooker: 4-quart

8 boneless, skinless chicken breast
    halves
0.7-oz. envelope dry Italian salad
    dressing mix
¼ cup water
8-oz. pkg. cream cheese, softened
10¾-oz. can cream of chicken soup
4-oz. can mushrooms, drained

1. Place chicken in greased slow
cooker. Combine salad dressing
mix and water. Pour over chicken.
2. Cover and cook on high 1 hour
and then on low 3 to 4 hours.
3. In saucepan, combine cream
cheese and soup. Heat slightly to
melt cream cheese. Stir in mushrooms. Pour over chicken.
4. Cover and cook on low 1 hour
more.
5. Serve over noodles or rice.

15-minute prep • entertaining

Chicken at a Whim

makes 6 to 8 servings
ideal slow cooker: 5-quart

6 boneless, skinless chicken breast
    halves
1 small onion, sliced
1 cup dry white wine, chicken broth,
    or water
15-oz. can chicken broth
2 cups water
6-oz. can sliced ripe olives,
    undrained
1 6-oz. jar marinated artichoke
    hearts, undrained
5 garlic cloves, minced
1 cup uncooked elbow macaroni or
    small shells
1-oz. envelope dry savory garlic soup
    mix
1 cup small grape tomatoes
    (optional)

1. Place chicken in slow cooker.
Spread onion over chicken.
2. Combine remaining ingredients
except garlic soup mix and grape
tomatoes and pour over chicken.
Sprinkle with garlic soup mix.
3. Cover and cook on high 1 hour
and then on low 3½ hours. Stir in
grape tomatoes 30 minutes before
serving, if desired.

Chicken and Bean Torta

Chicken and Bean Torta

makes 6 servings
ideal slow cooker: 4- or 5-quart

1 lb. boneless, skinless chicken
    breasts
1 medium onion, chopped
½ tsp. garlic salt
¼ tsp. black pepper
15-oz. can ranch-style black beans,
    drained
15-oz. can diced tomatoes with
    green chilies
4 8-inch tortillas
1½ cups shredded cheddar cheese
1 cup shredded lettuce
½ cup diced tomato
Salsa (optional)
Sour cream (optional)

1. Cut chicken in small pieces.
Brown with onion in a non-stick
skillet. Drain well.
2. Season chicken mixture with
garlic salt and pepper. Stir in
beans and tomatoes.
3. Place wide strips of foil on bottom and up sides of slow cooker
forming an X. Spray foil and
cooker lightly with cooking spray.
4. Place 1 tortilla on bottom of
cooker. Top with one-third of
chicken mixture and one-fourth of
the cheese.
5. Repeat layers, ending with a
tortilla sprinkled with cheese
on top.
6. Cover and cook on low 4 to
5 hours. Cool 10 minutes in slow
cooker.
7. Carefully remove to serving
platter using foil strips as handles.
Gently pull out foil and discard.
8. Top with lettuce and tomato.
Cut into wedges and serve with
salsa and sour cream, if desired.

Chicken Stroganoff

makes 4 servings
ideal slow cooker: 3-quart

4 boneless, skinless chicken breast
    halves, cubed
2 Tbsp. butter, melted
0.7-oz. envelope dry Italian salad
    dressing mix
8-oz. pkg. cream cheese, softened
10¾-oz. can cream of chicken soup

1. Place chicken, melted butter,
and dressing mix in slow cooker.
Stir together gently.
2. Cover and cook on high 1 hour
and then on low 4 to 5 hours.
3. Stir in cream cheese and soup.
Cover and cook on low 30 minutes
more or until heated through.
4. Serve over cooked rice or
noodles.

Cape Breton Chicken

makes 5 servings
ideal slow cooker: 4-quart

4 boneless, skinless chicken breast
    halves, cubed
1 medium onion, chopped
1 medium-size green bell pepper,
    chopped
1 cup celery, chopped
1 qt. stewed or crushed tomatoes
1 cup water
½ cup tomato paste
2 Tbsp. Worcestershire sauce
2 Tbsp. brown sugar
1 tsp. black pepper

1. Combine all ingredients in slow
cooker. Cover and cook on high
1 hour and then on low 6 hours.
2. Serve over rice.

Chicken Reuben Bake

makes 4 servings
ideal slow cooker: 4-quart

4 boneless, skinless chicken breast
    halves
2-lb. bag sauerkraut, drained and
    rinsed
4 to 5 slices Swiss cheese
1¼ cups Thousand Island salad
    dressing
2 Tbsp. chopped fresh parsley

1. Place chicken in slow cooker.
Layer sauerkraut over chicken
and top with cheese. Spoon salad
dressing over cheese and sprinkle
with parsley.
2. Cover and cook on high 1 hour
and then on low 5 to 7 hours.

Chicken Sweet Chicken

makes 6 to 8 servings
ideal slow cooker: 3-quart

2 medium-size sweet potatoes,
    peeled and cut into ¼-inch thick
    slices
8 boneless, skinless chicken thighs
8-oz. jar orange marmalade
¼ cup water
¼ to ½ tsp. salt
½ tsp. pepper

1. Place sweet potato slices in slow
cooker.
2. Rinse and dry chicken pieces.
Arrange on top of sweet potatoes.
Spoon marmalade over chicken
and potatoes; drizzle water over
all. Season with salt and pepper.
3. Cover and cook on high 1 hour
and then on low 4 to 5 hours or
until potatoes and chicken are
tender.

Chicken, Polenta, and Mushroom Alfredo Lasagna

entertaining • kid-friendly

Chicken, Polenta, and Mushroom Alfredo Lasagna

makes 6 servings
ideal slow cooker: 5-quart

2 3.5-oz. pkgs. fresh shiitake mushrooms

8-oz. pkg. sliced fresh mushrooms

1 medium onion, cut in half crosswise and sliced vertically

3 Tbsp. olive oil

1½ 16-oz. jars Alfredo sauce (we used Classico)

¼ cup dry white wine or 1 to 2 Tbsp. dry sherry

½ tsp. freshly ground pepper

¼ tsp. ground nutmeg

2 17-oz. tubes pesto-flavored or plain polenta, cut into ½-inch slices (we used Marjon Basil and Garlic Polenta)

1 cup freshly grated Parmesan cheese

2 cups cooked diced chicken thighs and breasts

Fresh basil sprigs (optional)

1. Remove and discard stems from shiitake mushrooms; thinly slice mushrooms. Sauté mushrooms and onion in hot oil in a large skillet over medium-high heat until onion is tender and liquid is absorbed.

2. Whisk together Alfredo sauce, wine, pepper, and nutmeg; stir into mushroom mixture. Spread 3 Tbsp. mushroom mixture in slow cooker. Layer one-third of polenta slices over sauce. Sprinkle ½ cup Parmesan cheese over polenta; top with half of remaining mushroom mixture and one-half of chicken. Layer one-third of polenta slices, remaining half of mushroom mixture and remaining half of chicken; top with remaining one-third of polenta slices. Sprinkle with remaining ½ cup Parmesan cheese.

3. Cover and cook on low 4 hours or until set. Remove lid, and let lasagna stand 15 minutes before serving. Garnish with fresh basil, if desired.

Chicken with Sesame Glaze

makes 4 servings
ideal slow cooker: 3-quart

1 Tbsp. hot chile sesame oil
4 large chicken thighs
3 garlic cloves, sliced
½ cup firmly packed brown sugar
3 Tbsp. soy sauce

1. Spread oil around the bottom of slow cooker.
2. Rinse chicken well and remove excess fat. Pat dry with paper towels. Place in slow cooker.
3. Sprinkle garlic slices over top of chicken. Crumble brown sugar over top. Drizzle with soy sauce.
4. Cover and cook on high 1 hour and then on low 3 to 7 hours or until thighs are tender.

serving tip:

: • Serve with hot cooked rice pre-
: pared with cooking liquid from
: slow cooker in place of water.

Thai Chicken

makes 6 servings
ideal slow cooker: 4-quart

6 skinless chicken thighs
¾ cup mild, medium, or hot salsa
¼ cup chunky peanut butter
1 Tbsp. soy sauce
2 Tbsp. lime juice
1 tsp. grated fresh gingerroot (optional)
2 Tbsp. chopped fresh cilantro (optional)
1 Tbsp. dry-roasted peanuts, chopped (optional)

1. Place chicken in slow cooker.
2. In a bowl, mix together remaining ingredients except cilantro and chopped peanuts. Pour salsa mixture over chicken.
3. Cover and cook on high 1 hour and then on low 7 to 8 hours or until chicken is tender.
4. Skim off any fat. Remove chicken to a platter and serve topped with sauce. Sprinkle with peanuts and cilantro, if desired.
5. Serve over cooked rice.

variation:

: • Vegetarians can substitute
: 2 15-oz. cans of white beans
: and perhaps some tofu for the
: chicken.

Chickenetti

makes 10 servings
ideal slow cooker: 6- or 7-quart

1 cup chicken broth
16-oz. pkg. spaghetti, cooked
4 to 6 cups cubed and cooked turkey or chicken
10¾-oz. can cream of mushroom soup or cream of celery soup
1 cup water
¼ cup green bell pepper, chopped
½ cup diced celery
½ tsp. black pepper
1 medium onion, grated
½ lb. white or yellow American cheese, cubed

1. Pour chicken broth into slow cooker. Add spaghetti and chicken.
2. In large bowl, combine soup and water until smooth. Stir in remaining ingredients; pour into slow cooker.
3. Cover and cook on low 2 to 3 hours.

Winter Squash and
White Bean Stew

hearty meatless mains

Winter Squash and White Bean Stew

makes 6 servings
ideal slow cooker: 4- or 5-quart

1 cup chopped onion
1 Tbsp. olive oil
½ tsp. ground cumin
¼ tsp. salt
¼ tsp. cinnamon
1 garlic clove, minced
3 cups peeled, cubed butternut
  squash
1½ cups chicken broth
19-oz. can cannellini beans,
  drained
14½-oz. can diced tomatoes,
  undrained
1 Tbsp. fresh cilantro leaves
Black pepper

1. Combine all ingredients except cilantro and black pepper in slow cooker.
2. Cover and cook on high 1 hour and then on low 2 to 3 hours. Garnish with cilantro leaves and black pepper.

15-minute prep
Black Bean and Corn Soup

makes 6 to 8 servings
ideal slow cooker: 4-quart

2 15-oz. cans black beans, drained
  and rinsed
14½-oz. can Mexican stewed
  tomatoes, undrained
14½-oz. can diced tomatoes,
  undrained
11-oz. can whole-kernel corn,
  drained
4 green onions, sliced
2 to 3 Tbsp. chili powder
1 tsp. ground cumin
½ tsp. dried minced garlic

1. Combine all ingredients in slow cooker. Cover and cook on high 5 to 6 hours.

tip:
• This soup tastes great with the addition of chopped celery and chopped green bell pepper.

kid-friendly
Broccoli, Potato, and Cheese Soup

makes 6 servings
ideal slow cooker: 3½-quart

2 cups cubed or diced potatoes
3 Tbsp. chopped onion
10-oz. pkg. frozen broccoli cuts,
  thawed
2 Tbsp. butter or margarine,
  melted
1 Tbsp. all-purpose flour
2 cups cubed pasteurized prepared
  cheese product
½ tsp. salt
5½ cups milk

1. Cook potatoes and onion in boiling water in saucepan until potatoes are crisp-tender. Drain well. Place in slow cooker.
2. Stir in remaining ingredients.
3. Cover and cook on low 4 hours.

Vegetable Paella

makes 7 servings
ideal slow cooker: 3½- or 4-quart

2 cups uncooked converted rice
(we used Uncle Ben's)
1 cup chopped onion
1 cup chopped green bell pepper
¼ cup chopped drained oil-packed
sun-dried tomatoes
1½ Tbsp. sun-dried tomato oil
1 tsp. salt
14½ oz. can Mexican-style stewed
tomatoes, undrained and
chopped
7.25-oz. jar roasted red bell
peppers, drained and chopped
4 garlic cloves, chopped
2 14½-oz. cans vegetable broth
(we used Swanson)
½-gram pkg. saffron threads
(1 tsp.)
16-oz. can chickpeas, rinsed and
drained
14-oz. can quartered artichoke
hearts, drained
1 cup frozen green peas

1. Place first 9 ingredients in slow
cooker; stir well. Combine broth
and saffron. Add to slow cooker;
stir well. Cover and cook on low
4 hours or until rice is tender and
liquid is absorbed.
2. Stir in chickpeas, artichoke
hearts, and green peas. Cover and
cook 15 minutes more.

Enchilada Casserole

makes 6 servings
ideal slow cooker: 3½-quart

3 Tbsp. diced green chilies, divided
½ cup salsa
¼ cup chopped green onions
¼ cup chopped fresh cilantro
15-oz. can black beans, rinsed and
drained
11-oz. can corn with red and green
peppers (we used Mexicorn),
drained
10-oz. can enchilada sauce
8½-oz. pkg. corn muffin mix
½ cup egg substitute
2 Tbsp. chopped bottled roasted
red bell pepper
1½ cups shredded Monterey jack
cheese
6 Tbsp. sour cream
1½ tsp. thinly sliced fresh cilantro

1. Place 2 Tbsp. green chilies and
next 6 ingredients in slow cooker;
stir well. Cover and cook on low
4 hours.
2. Combine remaining 1 Tbsp.
green chilies, muffin mix, egg
substitute, and roasted bell pepper
in a bowl; stir well. Spoon batter
evenly over bean mixture in slow
cooker. Cover and cook 1 hour
more or until corn bread is done.
3. Sprinkle cheese over corn
bread. Cover and cook 5 minutes
more or until cheese melts.
Spoon casserole onto plates; top
each serving with sour cream
and sprinkle with thinly sliced
cilantro.

Asparagus, Onion, and Mushroom Strata

makes 6 servings
ideal slow cooker: 3½-quart

1 Tbsp. olive oil
1 medium-size red onion, halved
and thinly sliced (about
1½ cups)
1 cup sliced fresh mushrooms
1 lb. fresh asparagus spears
3 cups (½-inch) cubed French bread
½ cup grated Parmesan cheese,
divided
1¼ cups milk
1 cup egg substitute
¼ cup mayonnaise
1 tsp. salt
½ tsp. white pepper
⅛ tsp. ground cloves
½ cup shredded sharp cheddar
cheese

1. Heat oil in a large skillet over
medium-high heat. Add onion;
sauté 10 minutes or until golden
brown. Add mushrooms; sauté 5
minutes or until tender. Put onion
mixture in greased slow cooker.
2. Snap off tough ends of asparagus; remove scales with a knife or
vegetable peeler, if desired. Cut
each spear in half lengthwise;
cut each half into 2-inch pieces.
Add asparagus and bread to slow
cooker; toss well. Sprinkle with
¼ cup parmesan cheese.
3. Combine milk and next 5 ingredients; stir with a whisk until well
blended. Pour milk mixture evenly
over bread mixture; sprinkle with
remaining Parmesan cheese. Cover
and chill 8 hours or overnight.
4. Remove from refrigerator. Cook
on high 2½ to 3 hours. Sprinkle
with cheddar cheese; cover and
cook 5 minutes more or until
cheese melts. Serve immediately.

Parmesan, Spinach,
and Barley Casserole

healthy for you

Parmesan, Spinach, and Barley Casserole

makes 6 servings
ideal slow cooker: 4-quart

32-oz. container vegetable
   or chicken broth (we used
   Swanson)
16-oz. can red beans, rinsed and
   drained
8-oz. pkg. pre-sliced fresh
   mushrooms
1½ cups uncooked fine barley
1½ cups sliced leek
1 cup chopped onion
1 tsp. dried Italian seasoning
½ tsp. pepper
½ tsp. salt
6-oz. pkg. fresh baby spinach
¾ cup finely shredded fresh
   Parmesan cheese

1. Place first 9 ingredients in slow cooker; stir well. Cover and cook on high 3 hours.
2. Add spinach. Cover and cook 15 minutes more; stir well (spinach will wilt). Sprinkle each serving with cheese.

Creamy Corn Soup

soothing soups and stews

Creamy Corn Soup

makes 12 servings
ideal slow cooker: 5-quart

1 lb. bacon
4 cups diced potato
2 cups chopped onion
2 cups sour cream
2½ cups milk
2 10¾-oz. cans cream of chicken
    soup
2 15¼-oz. cans whole-kernel corn,
    undrained
Thinly sliced green onions

1. Cook bacon in a large skillet
until crisp. Drain well, crumble,
and set aside.
2. Add potato, onion, and a small
amount of water to skillet. Cook
15 minutes or until tender, stirring
occasionally. Drain. Transfer
potato, onion, and all but ½ cup
crumbled bacon to slow cooker.
(Refrigerate reserved bacon.)
3. Stir in sour cream, milk, soup,
and corn. Cover and cook on low
2 hours. Sprinkle green onions and
reserved bacon on each serving.

entertaining • for the holidays

Pumpkin Soup

makes 6 servings
ideal slow cooker: 3½-quart

¼ cup chopped green bell pepper
1 small onion, finely chopped
2 cups chicken broth
15-oz. can pumpkin puree
2 cups milk
⅛ tsp. dried thyme
¼ tsp. ground nutmeg
½ tsp. salt
2 Tbsp. cornstarch
¼ cup cold water
1 tsp. chopped fresh parsley
Ground nutmeg

1. Combine first 8 ingredients in
slow cooker. Cover and cook on
low 4 to 5 hours.
2. Combine cornstarch and water,
stirring until smooth. Stir into
soup. Cover and cook 10 minutes
more or until soup thickens.
3. Stir in fresh parsley just before
serving. Sprinkle individual servings with ground nutmeg.

Adirondack Soup

makes 12 servings
ideal slow cooker: 6-quart

2 qts. stewed tomatoes
3 1-lb. cans low-sodium vegetable
    broth
3 cups water
5 large carrots, chopped
1 large onion, chopped
4 celery ribs, chopped
2 tsp. dried basil
1 tsp. dried parsley
1 tsp. black pepper
2 dashes hot sauce (we used
    Tabasco)
3 cups frozen mixed vegetables,
    thawed

1. Combine all ingredients except
frozen vegetables in slow cooker.
Cover and cook on low 6 hours.
2. Stir in mixed vegetables. Cover
and cook 1 hour more.

Minestrone

makes 8 to 10 servings
ideal slow cooker: 5-quart

1 large onion, chopped
4 carrots, sliced
3 celery ribs, sliced
2 garlic cloves, minced
1 Tbsp. olive oil
6-oz. can tomato paste
14½-oz. can chicken, beef, or
    vegetable broth
24-oz. can pinto beans, undrained
10-oz. pkg. frozen green beans
2 to 3 cups chopped cabbage
1 medium zucchini, sliced
8 cups water
2 Tbsp. chopped fresh parsley
2 Tbsp. dried Italian seasoning
1 tsp. salt
½ tsp. pepper
¾ cup dry acini di pepe or other
    small pasta
Grated Parmesan or Asiago cheese

1. Sauté onion, carrots, celery, and garlic in oil until tender.
2. Combine vegetable mixture and remaining ingredients except pasta and cheese in slow cooker.
3. Cover and cook on high 4 to 5 hours or on low 8 to 9 hours, adding pasta 1 hour before cooking is complete.
4. Top individual servings with cheese.

Soup to Get Thin On

makes 20 servings
ideal slow cooker: 7-quart

3 48-oz. cans low-fat, low-sodium
    chicken broth
2 medium onions, chopped
5 celery ribs, chopped
5 parsnips, chopped
1 head cabbage, shredded
4 red or green bell peppers,
    chopped
8 ozs. fresh mushrooms, chopped
10-oz. pkg. frozen chopped
    spinach, thawed
10-oz. pkg. frozen broccoli florets,
    thawed
10-oz. pkg. frozen cauliflower
    florets, thawed
2 1-inch thick slices fresh
    gingerroot
14½-oz. can crushed tomatoes
1 Tbsp. black pepper
1 Tbsp. salt

1. Combine all ingredients in slow cooker. Cover and cook on low 6 to 8 hours.

Beef-Barley Vegetable Soup

makes 10 to 12 servings
ideal slow cooker: 8-quart

1 lb. ground beef
1½ qts. water
1 qt. stewed tomatoes
3 cups sliced carrot
1 cup diced celery
1 cup diced potato
1 cup diced onion
¾ cup quick-cook barley
3 tsp. beef bouillon granules or
    3 beef bouillon cubes
2 to 3 tsp. salt
¼ tsp. pepper

1. Brown ground beef in a large skillet over medium-high heat. Drain well. Transfer meat into slow cooker. Stir in remaining ingredients.
2. Cover and cook on high 4 to 5 hours or on low 8 to 10 hours.
3. Serve with fresh bread and cheese cubes.

Beef Goulash Vegetable Soup

makes 6 servings
ideal slow cooker: 4-quart

1 lb. lean ground beef
1 large onion, diced
2 celery ribs, chopped
8-oz. can tomato sauce
3 14½-oz. cans beef broth
10-oz. pkg. frozen green beans
1½ tsp. chili powder
1 tsp. paprika
½ tsp. black pepper
1½ cups flat wide noodles,
    uncooked

1. Sauté ground beef, onion, and celery in a skillet until meat is browned and vegetables are crisp-tender. Transfer to slow cooker.
2. Stir in tomato sauce, broth, green beans, chili powder, paprika, and black pepper.
3. Cover and cook on low 5 to 7 hours. Add wide noodles and cook 1 hour more.

Turkey-Zucchini Soup

makes 8 servings
ideal slow cooker: 4-quart

10-oz. pkg. frozen green beans,
    thawed
2 cups thinly sliced zucchini
2 cups chopped cooked turkey
8-oz. can tomato sauce
½ cup chopped onion
1 Tbsp. chicken bouillon granules
1 tsp. Worcestershire sauce
¼ tsp. salt
½ tsp. dried savory, crushed
Dash of black pepper
4 cups water
3 ozs. cream cheese, softened

1. Combine all ingredients except
cream cheese in slow cooker. Cover
and cook on high 2 to 3 hours.
2. Blend 1 cup hot soup with
cream cheese. Return cheese
mixture to slow cooker, stirring
well. Cover and cook 15 minutes
more or until hot.

Roasted Chicken Noodle Soup

makes 8 servings
ideal slow cooker: 5-quart

1 cup chopped onion
1 cup chopped carrot
1 cup chopped celery
1 garlic clove, minced
2 tsp. olive or canola oil
¼ tsp. all-purpose flour
½ tsp. dried oregano
½ tsp. dried thyme
¼ tsp. poultry seasoning
6 cups chicken broth
4 cups diced potato
½ tsp. salt
2 cups diced roasted chicken
2 cups uncooked wide egg noodles
1 cup evaporated milk

1. Cook onion, carrot, celery, and
garlic in hot oil in a large skillet
until tender. Stir in flour, oregano,
thyme, and poultry seasoning and
blend well. Pour mixture into slow
cooker.
2. Stir in broth, potato, and salt.
Cover and cook on low 5 to 6
hours or until potato is soft.
3. Stir in chicken, noodles, and
milk. Cover and cook 30 minutes
more or until noodles are tender.
Serve with crackers.

15-minute prep

Mediterranean Beef Stew

makes 4 servings
ideal slow cooker: 3½-quart

2 medium zucchini, cut into bite-
    size pieces
¾ lb. beef stew meat, cut into
    ½-inch pieces
2 14½-oz. cans Italian-style diced
    tomatoes, undrained
½ tsp. pepper (optional)
2-inch stick cinnamon or ¼ tsp.
    ground cinnamon

1. Place zucchini in the bottom of
slow cooker.
2. Add beef and remaining
ingredients in the order listed.
3. Cover and cook on high 3 to 5
hours or until the meat is tender.

cooking tip:

• You can also cook the stew on
high 1 hour and then on low
7 hours more or until meat is
tender.

15-minute prep

Golfer's Stew

makes 4 to 5 servings
ideal slow cooker: 4-quart

1 lb. beef stew meat, cubed
12-oz. jar beef gravy or beef and
    mushroom gravy
6 medium potatoes, cut in ½-inch
    chunks
6 carrots, cut in thick slices
3 celery ribs, cut in thick slices
2 to 3 onions, cut in wedges

1. Place all ingredients in slow
cooker. Stir together gently.
2. Cover and cook on high 1 hour.
Turn heat to low and cook 6 hours
more.

kid-friendly • make-ahead

Pixie's Chicken Stew

makes 8 to 10 servings
ideal slow cooker: 6-quart

2- to 3-lb. chicken, cut up
2 qts. water
2.1-oz. pkg. dry chicken noodle
    soup
2 chicken bouillon cubes
15-oz. can whole-kernel corn,
    undrained
1 Tbsp. dried onion flakes
½ tsp. dried thyme

1. Place chicken in slow cooker
and add water. Cover and cook on
high 3 to 4 hours. Remove chicken
and cool.
2. Strain broth through a wire-
meshed strainer into a large bowl,
discarding solids. Skin, bone, and
cut chicken into bite-size pieces.
Return chicken and broth to slow
cooker.
3. Stir in remaining ingredients.
Cover and cook on high 2 hours.

Taco Chili

kid-friendly

Taco Chili

makes 8 servings
ideal slow cooker: 5-quart

1 lb. ground beef
1 onion, chopped
1-oz. dry ranch-style salad
    dressing mix
1.25-oz. envelope taco
    seasoning mix
3 12-oz. cans diced tomatoes with
    green chilies, undrained

2 24-oz. cans pinto beans,
    undrained
24-oz. can hominy, drained
14.5-oz. can stewed tomatoes,
    undrained
2 cups water
Accompaniments: sour cream, fresh
    cilantro, tortilla chips (optional)

1. Brown ground beef and onion
in a large skillet over medium-high
heat. Drain well. Transfer meat
mixture to slow cooker.

2. Stir in remaining ingredients
except accompaniments.
3. Cover and cook on low 4 hours.
Serve with accompaniments, if
desired.

cooking tip:

• Increase or decrease the amount
of water you add to make the chili
either soup-like or stew-like.

Spicy Chili

makes 4 to 6 servings
ideal slow cooker: 4-quart

½ lb. Italian sausage, casings
   removed
½ lb. ground beef
½ cup chopped onion
½ lb. fresh mushrooms, sliced
2 Tbsp. chopped celery
2 Tbsp. chopped green bell pepper
1 cup salsa
16-oz. can tomato juice
6-oz. can tomato paste
½ tsp. sugar
½ tsp. salt
½ tsp. dried oregano
½ tsp. Worcestershire sauce
¼ tsp. dried basil
¼ tsp. pepper

1. Brown sausage, ground beef, and onion in a large skillet over medium-high heat, stirring often until meat crumbles and is no longer pink. Add mushrooms, celery, and bell pepper during the last 3 minutes of cooking. Drain well and transfer to slow cooker.
2. Stir in remaining ingredients. Cover and cook on high 2 to 3 hours.

variation:

: • For an even heartier chili,
: add any or all of the following
: ingredients to Step 2: 1 tsp. chili
: powder, 1 tsp. ground cumin,
: 15-oz. can black beans, 15-oz.
: can whole-kernel corn.

White Chili

makes 6 to 8 servings
ideal slow cooker: 4-quart

15-oz. can garbanzo beans,
   undrained
15-oz. can small Northern beans,
   undrained
15-oz. can pinto beans, undrained
2 1-lb. bags frozen corn
1½ cups shredded cooked chicken
2 Tbsp. minced onion
1 red bell pepper, diced
1 Tbsp. minced garlic
1 Tbsp. ground cumin
½ tsp. salt
½ tsp. dried oregano
2 15-oz. cans chicken broth
Toppings: sour cream, green onion
   slices, shredded cheddar cheese

1. Combine all ingredients in slow cooker.
2. Cover and cook on high 4 to 5 hours or on low 8 to 10 hours.
3. Serve with toppings and tortilla chips.

Dawn's Sirloin No-Bean Chili

makes 10 servings
ideal slow cooker: 3-quart

1 lb. sirloin steak, trimmed of
   all fat
2 Tbsp. canola oil
2 large onions, chopped
16-oz. can chopped tomatoes,
   undrained
8-oz. can tomato paste
1½ cups beef broth
½ tsp. salt
¼ tsp. black pepper

1. Cut steak into 1-inch pieces. Cook steak in hot oil in a large skillet over medium-high heat until browned.
2. Combine steak and remaining ingredients in slow cooker.
3. Cover and cook on low 8 hours.

Chicken Clam Chowder

makes 12 servings
ideal slow cooker: 6-quart

¼ lb. bacon, diced
¼ lb. lean ham, cubed
2 cups chopped onion
2 cups diced celery
¼ tsp. pepper
2 cups diced potato
2 cups diced cooked chicken
4 tsp. chicken bouillon granules
   mixed with 4 cups water
2 8-oz. bottles clam juice
1-lb. can whole-kernel corn,
   drained and rinsed
¼ to ½ cup water
¾ cup all-purpose flour
3 cups milk
1½ cups half-and-half
4 cups shredded cheddar or
   Monterey jack cheese
½ cup whipping cream
2 Tbsp. chopped fresh parsley

1. Cook bacon, ham, onion, and celery in a skillet until bacon is crisp and onions and celery are tender. Stir in pepper.
2. Combine bacon mixture, potato, and next 5 ingredients in slow cooker.
3. Cover and cook on high 3 to 4 hours or on low 6 to 8 hours.
4. Whisk flour into milk and half-and-half. Stir into soup, along with cheese, whipping cream, and parsley. Cover and cook on high 1 hour more.

Golden Cauliflower

side-dish sensations

editor's favorite
Golden Cauliflower

makes 4 to 6 servings
ideal slow cooker: 3-quart

1 small head fresh cauliflower, trimmed
Salt and pepper to taste
10¾-oz. can cheddar cheese soup
4 slices bacon, crisply fried and crumbled

1. Place cauliflower in slow cooker, stem side down. Sprinkle with salt and pepper.
2. Spoon soup over cauliflower.
3. Cover and cook on high 1½ hours or on low 4 to 5 hours or until cauliflower is tender. Sprinkle with bacon before serving.

15-minute prep
Green Beans Au Gratin

makes 12 to 14 servings
ideal slow cooker: 4-quart

2 lbs. frozen green beans
1 to 2 cups cubed pasteurized prepared cheese product (we used Velveeta)
½ cup chopped onion
½ cup milk
1 Tbsp. all-purpose flour

1. Combine beans, cheese, and onion in slow cooker; stir well.
2. Place milk in a jar with a tight-fitting lid; add flour. Top with lid and shake jar until mixture is smooth. Add flour mixture to slow cooker, stirring well.
3. Cover and cook on low 5 to 6 hours or until beans are fully cooked and heated through.

Greek-Style Green Beans

makes 6 servings
ideal slow cooker: 4-quart

20 ozs. frozen green beans
2 cups tomato sauce
2 tsp. dried onion flakes (optional)
Pinch of dried marjoram or oregano
Pinch of ground nutmeg
Pinch of ground cinnamon
Feta cheese (optional)

1. Combine all ingredients except cheese in slow cooker, stirring well.
2. Cover and cook on low 2 to 4 hours if the beans are defrosted or 3 to 5 hours if the beans are frozen. Top with feta cheese before serving, if desired.

Candied Carrots

makes 3 to 4 servings
ideal slow cooker: 3-quart

1 lb. carrots, cut in 1-inch pieces
½ tsp. salt
¼ cup water
2 Tbsp. butter or margarine
½ cup firmly packed light brown
  sugar
2 Tbsp. chopped nuts

1. Place carrots in slow cooker.
Sprinkle with salt.
2. Add water; cover and cook on
high 2 to 3 hours or until carrots
are just tender. Drain.
3. Stir in butter and sprinkle with
sugar.
4. Cover and cook 30 minutes
more. Sprinkle with nuts just
before serving.

editor's favorite

Peppered
Corn on the Cob

makes 6 servings
ideal slow cooker: 5-quart

6 Tbsp. butter, softened
4 garlic cloves, pressed
6 ears fresh corn, husks removed
1 tsp. freshly ground black pepper
½ tsp. salt
12 fully cooked slices bacon (we
  used Ready Crisp Bacon)
½ cup chicken broth
1 jalapeño pepper, minced

1. Combine butter and garlic in
a small bowl. Rub garlic butter
evenly over ears of corn. Sprinkle
evenly with pepper and salt. Wrap
each ear of corn with 2 slices
bacon and secure with toothpicks.
Place corn in slow cooker. Add

broth and jalapeño pepper.
2. Cover and cook on low 3 to 4
hours or until corn is tender.
Remove bacon before serving, if
desired.

cooking tip:

• Instead of wrapping bacon
around each ear of corn, simply
chop the bacon and sprinkle
on top of the corn in the slow
cooker.

15-minute prep

Corny Cornbread

makes 8 servings
ideal slow cooker: 4-quart

1 egg
½ cup sour cream
½ cup butter, melted
2 14¾-oz. cans cream-style corn
8½-oz. pkg. corn bread mix (we
  used Jiffy)

1. Spray inside of slow cooker with
cooking spray.
2. Mix all ingredients together in
a bowl. Spoon into greased slow
cooker.
3. Cover and cook on high 3 hours
and 45 minutes.

Creamed Hominy

makes 4 servings
ideal slow cooker: 3-quart

1½ cups half-and-half, divided
15-oz. can hominy, drained
2 Tbsp. sugar
3 Tbsp. butter, softened
1 tsp. salt
2 Tbsp. water

1. Combine 1 cup half-and-half

and remaining ingredients in slow
cooker, stirring well.
2. Cover and cook on low 3 to 4
hours. If mixture appears dry after
3 hours, stir in an additional ¼ to
½ cup half-and-half.

Mushrooms in
Red Wine

makes 4 servings
ideal slow cooker: 2-quart

1 lb. fresh mushrooms
4 garlic cloves, chopped
¼ cup chopped onion
1 Tbsp. olive oil
1 cup red wine

1. Combine all ingredients in slow
cooker. Cover and cook on low
4 to 6 hours.

serving tip:

• Mushrooms in Red Wine makes
a perfect side dish with grilled
steaks or roast beef.

Stuffed Peppers

makes 4 servings
ideal slow cooker: 5-quart

4 medium-size green, yellow, or
  red bell peppers
1 cup cooked rice
15-oz. can chili beans with chili
  gravy
1 cup shredded cheddar cheese,
  divided
14½-oz. can petite diced tomatoes
  with onion, celery, and green
  pepper, undrained

1. Remove top, membranes, and
seeds from each pepper, keeping
peppers whole.

2. Combine rice, beans, and half the cheese in a bowl; stir well. Spoon rice mixture evenly into peppers.

3. Pour tomatoes into slow cooker. Place stuffed peppers, cut sides up, in slow cooker on top of tomatoes. (Do not stack stuffed peppers.)

4. Cover and cook on high 3 hours.

5. Carefully lift peppers out of slow cooker and place on a serving platter. Spoon hot tomatoes over stuffed peppers. Sprinkle with remaining cheese.

Parmesan Potato Wedges

5 ingredients or less

Scalloped Potatoes

makes 6 to 8 servings
ideal slow cooker: 4-quart

1 pt. half-and-half

½ cup butter, melted

30-oz. pkg. frozen hash brown potatoes

1 tsp. garlic powder

¼ tsp. pepper

1-lb. loaf pasteurized prepared cheese product, cubed (we used Velveeta)

1. Spray interior of slow cooker with cooking spray.

2. Place all ingredients except cheese in slow cooker. Stir together until well mixed.

3. Cover and cook on low 4 to 5 hours or until potatoes are tender and cooked through.

4. Stir in cheese. Cover and cook 30 minutes more or until cheese is melted. Stir just before serving.

15-minute prep

Parmesan Potato Wedges

makes 6 servings
ideal slow cooker: 3-quart

2 lbs. small red potatoes, cut in ½-inch wedges

¼ cup chopped onion

2 Tbsp. butter, cut in small pieces

1½ Tbsp. chopped fresh oregano or 1½ tsp. dried oregano

¼ cup freshly grated Parmesan cheese

1. Layer potato, onion, butter, and oregano in slow cooker.

2. Cover and cook on high 2 hours or until potatoes are tender.

3. Spoon into serving dish and sprinkle with cheese.

Bacon Hash Browns

makes 5 to 6 servings
ideal slow cooker: 4-quart

¼ lb. bacon
6 cups frozen hash brown
  potatoes, partially thawed
1 cup mayonnaise
½ cup processed cheese spread (we
  used Cheese Whiz)

1. Cook bacon in a large skillet
until crisp. Drain well. Crumble
and set aside.
2. Spray interior of slow cooker
with cooking spray.
3. Measure out ¼ cup crumbled
bacon and reserve. Place remaining bacon, hash brown potatoes,
mayonnaise, and cheese spread in
slow cooker, stirring well.
4. Cover and cook on low 4 hours.
5. Sprinkle with reserved bacon
just before serving.

Satisfyingly Creamy Potatoes

makes 8 to 10 servings
ideal slow cooker: 5-quart

1 pt. sour cream
10¾-oz. can cream of chicken soup
2 cups cubed pasteurized prepared
  cheese product (we used
  Velveeta)
½ cup chopped onion
30-oz. pkg. frozen hash brown
  potatoes

1. Spray interior of slow cooker
with cooking spray.
2. Combine all ingredients in the
slow cooker, stirring well.
3. Cover and cook on low 3 to 4
hours or until potatoes are tender
and cooked through.

Easy Olive Bake

Easy Olive Bake

makes 8 servings
ideal slow cooker: 3-quart

1 cup uncooked rice
1 medium onion, chopped
½ cup butter or margarine, melted
14½-oz. can diced tomatoes,
  drained
2 cups water
1 cup pitted black olives, quartered
½ to ¾ tsp. salt
½ tsp. chili powder
1 Tbsp. Worcestershire sauce
4-oz. can mushrooms, undrained
½ cup freshly grated Parmesan
  cheese

1. Rinse and drain rice. Place in
slow cooker. Stir in remaining
ingredients except cheese.
2. Cover and cook on high 1 hour.
Turn heat to low and cook 2 hours
more or until rice is tender.
3. Top with cheese before serving.

Acorn Squash

makes 4 to 6 servings
ideal slow cooker: 4- or 5-quart

3 small acorn squash
¼ cup butter or margarine
½ to 1 tsp. ground cinnamon
¼ tsp. salt
2 Tbsp. brown sugar or maple
  syrup

1. Cut squash in half; scoop out and discard seeds. Place squash in slow cooker.
2. Cover and cook on low 7 to 8 hours or until squash is tender.
3. Remove squash from slow cooker and cool.
4. Scoop squash pulp into a large bowl. Add remaining ingredients and mash with a potato masher to desired consistency.

Sweet Potato Stuffing

makes 8 servings
ideal slow cooker: 3-quart

¼ cup butter
½ cup chopped celery
½ cup chopped onion
6 cups dry bread cubes
1 large sweet potato, cooked,
  peeled, and cubed
½ cup chicken broth
¼ cup chopped pecans
½ tsp. poultry seasoning
½ tsp. rubbed sage
½ tsp. salt
¼ tsp. pepper

1. Melt butter in a skillet over low heat. Add celery and onion and sauté until tender. Pour into greased slow cooker.
2. Add remaining ingredients, tossing gently until well combined.
3. Cover and cook on low 4 hours.

Pineapple Stuffing

makes 4 to 6 servings
ideal slow cooker: 4-quart

½ cup butter, softened
½ cup sugar
3 eggs
20-oz. can crushed pineapple,
  drained
6 slices day-old bread, cubed

1. Combine butter and sugar in a large mixing bowl.
2. Add eggs 1 at a time, mixing thoroughly after each addition.
3. Stir in drained pineapple. Fold in bread cubes. Spoon mixture into slow cooker.
4. Cover and cook on low 3 to 4 hours or until heated through.
5. Let stand 15 minutes before serving.

serving suggestion:

• Sprinkle each serving with grated extra-sharp cheddar cheese, if desired.

Slow-Cooker Dressing

makes 16 servings
ideal slow cooker: 6-quart

2 8½-oz. pkgs. corn bread mix (we
  used Jiffy)
8 slices day-old bread, torn
4 eggs
1 onion, chopped
½ cup chopped celery
2 10¾-oz. cans cream of chicken
  soup
2 cups chicken broth
1 tsp. salt
½ tsp. pepper
1½ Tbsp. rubbed sage or poultry
  seasoning
½ to ¾ cup butter or margarine,
  cut in small pieces

1. Prepare corn bread according to package instructions.
2. Crumble corn bread in a large mixing bowl. Add bread, eggs, onion, celery, soup, broth, salt, pepper, and sage; stir well. Spoon mixture into greased slow cooker. Top with butter.
3. Cover and cook on high 2 to 4 hours or on low 3 to 8 hours.

Cherry Cobbler

sweet inspirations

Cherry Cobbler

makes 4 to 6 servings
ideal slow cooker: 3-quart

21-oz. can cherry pie filling
1¾ cups yellow cake mix
1 egg
3 Tbsp. evaporated milk
½ tsp. ground cinnamon
Vanilla ice cream

1. Lightly spray inside of slow cooker with cooking spray.
2. Place pie filling in slow cooker. Cover and cook on high 30 minutes.
3. Meanwhile, mix together remaining ingredients except ice cream in a medium bowl until combined. Spoon batter over hot pie filling.
4. Cover and cook on low 3 to 5 hours more or until a toothpick inserted in center of topping comes out clean. Serve warm or at room temperature with vanilla ice cream.

Apple Grunt

makes 9 servings
ideal slow cooker: 4-quart

5 medium apples, peeled and cut in wedges
½ cup sugar
⅓ cup all-purpose flour
¼ tsp. apple pie spice
2 cups biscuit and baking mix (we used Bisquick)
¾ cup milk
3 Tbsp. sugar
3 Tbsp. butter or margarine, melted
3 cups vanilla low-fat frozen yogurt

1. Coat inside of slow cooker with cooking spray. Combine apples, ½ cup sugar, flour, and apple pie spice in slow cooker; stir well.
2. Combine biscuit mix, milk, 3 Tbsp. sugar, and butter in a bowl; stir just until moist. Spoon dough over apple mixture.
3. Cover and cook on low 6 hours. Serve warm with frozen yogurt.

5 ingredients or less • entertaining

Caramel Apples

makes 4 servings
ideal slow cooker: 3-quart

4 large tart apples, cored
14-oz. jar caramel sauce
½ cup apple juice
1 tsp. apple pie spice

1. Remove peel from top one-third of whole apples.
2. Place apples in slow cooker, making sure that each one sits flat on bottom of the cooker. Fill the center of each apple with one-fourth of the caramel sauce.
3. Pour apple juice around apples in the bottom of cooker. Sprinkle apples with apple pie spice.
4. Cover and cook on high 2 to 3 hours.

serving idea:

• Serve with butter pecan ice cream and shortbread cookies.

Baked Custard

makes 4 servings
ideal slow cooker: 4- or 5-quart

2 cups whole milk
3 eggs, slightly beaten
⅓ cup sugar
1 tsp. vanilla extract
¼ tsp. cinnamon
½ tsp. sugar

1. Heat milk in a small saucepan until a skin forms on top. Remove from heat and let cool slightly.
2. Whisk together eggs, ⅓ cup sugar, and vanilla in a large mixing bowl. Slowly stir cooled milk into egg mixture.
3. Pour mixture into a greased 1-qt. baking dish that will fit inside your slow cooker or into a baking insert designed to fit slow cooker.
4. Mix cinnamon and ½ tsp. sugar. Sprinkle over custard mixture.
5. Cover baking dish or baking insert with foil. Set dish on a metal rack or trivet in slow cooker. Pour hot water into slow cooker around dish to a depth of 1 inch.
6. Cover and cook on high 2 to 3 hours or until custard sets. Serve warm.

cooking tip:

• Custard is set and done when the blade of a knife inserted in center of custard comes out clean.

Pumpkin Pie Dessert

makes 3 servings
ideal slow cooker: 5- or 6-quart

19-oz. can pumpkin pie filling
12-oz. can evaporated milk
2 eggs, lightly beaten
1 cup gingersnap cookie crumbs

1. Combine pie filling, milk, and eggs in a mixing bowl; stir until thoroughly blended.
2. Pour mixture into an ungreased baking insert designed to fit slow cooker.
3. Place filled baking insert into slow cooker. Cover the insert with its lid or with 8 paper towels.
4. Carefully pour hot water into slow cooker around the baking insert to a depth of 1 inch.
5. Cover and cook on high 3 to 4 hours or until the blade of a knife inserted in center of custard comes out clean.
6. Remove baking insert from slow cooker. Uncover and sprinkle dessert with cookie crumbs. Serve warm.

Apple-Nut Bread Pudding

makes 6 to 8 servings
ideal slow cooker: 4-quart

8 slices raisin bread, cubed
2 to 3 medium-size tart apples, peeled and sliced
1 cup chopped pecans, toasted
1 cup sugar
1 tsp. ground cinnamon
½ tsp. ground nutmeg
3 eggs, lightly beaten
2 cups half-and-half
¼ cup apple juice
¼ cup butter or margarine, melted

1. Combine bread cubes, apples, and pecans in greased slow cooker.
2. Combine sugar, cinnamon, and nutmeg in a bowl. Add remaining ingredients; whisk until blended. Pour egg mixture over bread mixture.
3. Cover and cook on low 3 to 4 hours or until the blade of a knife inserted in center of bread pudding comes out clean.

Chocolate Bread Pudding

makes 8 servings
ideal slow cooker: 3- or 4-quart

1 cup semisweet chocolate morsels, divided
2½ cups milk
3 large egg whites
1 large egg
1 cup sugar
2 tsp. vanilla extract
8 ozs. French bread, cut into 1-inch cubes

1. Place ½ cup chocolate morsels in a medium bowl. Microwave at high 30 seconds or until chocolate melts. Cool slightly.
2. Place milk in a 1-qt. glass liquid measuring cup or glass bowl. Microwave at high 1 minute or until barely warm. Gradually add milk to chocolate, stirring with a whisk until well blended. Let cool.
3. Whisk in egg whites and egg. Stir in sugar and vanilla.
4. Place bread cubes and remaining ½ cup chocolate morsels in slow cooker. Pour milk mixture over bread, tossing to moisten bread.
5. Cover and cook on low 4 hours or until pudding is slightly puffed and set.

Tapioca Parfait

makes 12 servings
ideal slow cooker: 4-quart

¾ cup large pearl tapioca
⅓ cup sugar
Dash salt
4 cups water
1 cup green seedless grapes, cut in half
1 cup pineapple tidbits, drained
1 cup chopped fresh strawberries
1 cup frozen whipped topping, thawed
Whole strawberries (optional)

1. Combine tapioca, sugar, salt, and water in slow cooker; stir well.
2. Cover and cook on high 3 hours or until tapioca pearls are almost translucent.
3. Cool completely in refrigerator.
4. Stir in grapes, pineapple, and chopped strawberries. Fold in whipped topping. Serve in chilled parfait glasses. Garnish with whole strawberries, if desired.

Pineapple Tapioca

makes 4 to 6 servings
ideal slow cooker: 3-quart

2½ cups water
2½ cups pineapple juice
½ cup small pearl tapioca
¾ to 1 cup sugar
15-oz. can crushed pineapple, undrained

1. Mix first 4 ingredients together in slow cooker.
2. Cover and cook on high 3 hours.
3. Stir in crushed pineapple. Transfer mixture to a bowl; cover and chill several hours before serving.

Tapioca Parfait

entertaining

Dessert Fondue

makes about 3 cups
ideal slow cooker: 4-quart

1 Tbsp. butter
8 1-oz. milk chocolate candy bars, coarsely chopped
8 1-oz. semisweet chocolate candy bars, coarsely chopped
30 large marshmallows
⅓ cup milk
1 cup whipping cream

1. Grease slow cooker with 1 Tbsp. butter. Preheat slow cooker on high 10 minutes.
2. Combine candy bars, marshmallows, and milk in a bowl. Pour candy bar mixture into slow cooker.
3. Cover and cook on low 30 minutes. Stir; cover and cook 30 minutes more. Stir until blended.
4. Stir in whipping cream. Cover and cook on low 1 hour more.
5. Turn heat to warm setting and serve from the slow cooker with small squares of pound cake or angel food cake, banana slices, and pretzels for dipping.

Peanut Butter Cake

makes 6 servings
ideal slow cooker: 4-quart

2 cups yellow cake mix

⅓ cup crunchy peanut butter

½ cup water

1 large egg

Ready-to-spread chocolate frosting

Chopped peanuts and crumbled
   peanut butter cups (optional)

1. Line slow cooker with a disposable slow cooker heavy-duty plastic liner and coat inside with cooking spray. Set aside.

2. Combine first 4 ingredients in a large mixing bowl. Beat with electric mixer 2 minutes. Pour batter into prepared slow cooker.

3. Cover and cook on high 30 to 45 minutes or until toothpick inserted in center of cake comes out clean. Cool cake in slow cooker 15 minutes.

4. Carefully lift cake from slow cooker using plastic liner. Remove and discard plastic liner. Cool cake completely on a wire rack.

5. Cover top and sides with chocolate frosting. Sprinkle with peanuts and cups, if desired.

Black Forest Cake

makes 8 to 10 servings
ideal slow cooker: 4- or 5-quart

20-oz. can cherry pie filling
18.25-oz. pkg. butter-style
  chocolate cake mix

1. Preheat slow cooker on high 10 minutes.
2. Spray interior of baking insert designed to fit slow cooker with cooking spray.
3. Stir together pie filling and cake mix in a medium bowl until cake mix is thoroughly moistened. Spoon batter into insert.
4. Place filled baking insert in slow cooker. Cover the insert with its lid or with 8 paper towels.
5. Cover slow cooker and cook on high 1 hour and 45 minutes. Remove slow cooker lid and paper towels. Cook 30 minutes more or until a toothpick inserted in the center of the cake comes out clean.
6. Remove baking insert from cooker. Serve cake warm directly from the insert.

Dump Cake

makes 8 to 10 servings
ideal slow cooker: 3½- or 4-quart

20-oz. can crushed pineapple,
  undrained
21-oz. can blueberry or cherry pie
  filling
18.5-oz. pkg. yellow cake mix
Ground cinnamon
½ cup butter or margarine, cut in
  small pieces
1 cup chopped nuts
Vanilla ice cream

1. Grease bottom and sides of slow cooker.

2. Spread layers of pineapple, blueberry pie filling, and cake mix. Be careful not to mix the layers.
3. Sprinkle with cinnamon. Top with pieces of butter and nuts.
4. Cover and cook on high 2 to 3 hours.
5. Serve with vanilla ice cream.

Easy Autumn Cake

makes 8 servings
ideal slow cooker: 3½- or 4-quart

2 16-oz. cans sliced apples,
  undrained
18.25-oz. pkg. spice cake
  mix
½ cup butter, melted
½ cup chopped pecans

1. Spray interior of slow cooker with cooking spray.
2. Spoon apples and their juices into slow cooker, spreading evenly over the bottom.
3. Sprinkle with spice cake mix.
4. Pour melted butter over cake mix. Top with chopped pecans.
5. Cover and cook on low 3 to 5 hours or until a toothpick inserted in center of cake comes out clean.
6. Serve warm from slow cooker.

cooking tip:

• Be certain to select sliced apples instead of apple pie filling for this cool-weather dessert.

Peach and Walnut Cake

makes 10 to 12 servings
ideal slow cooker: 3½- or 4-quart

2 21-oz. cans peach pie filling
18.25-oz. pkg. yellow cake mix
½ cup butter, melted
⅓ cup chopped walnuts

1. Spray interior of slow cooker with cooking spray.
2. Spoon peach pie filling into slow cooker.
3. Combine cake mix and butter in a bowl; stir until well blended. Spoon batter over pie filling.
4. Sprinkle walnuts over top.
5. Cover and cook on low 3 to 5 hours or until a toothpick inserted into center comes out clean.

5 ingredients or less

Almost Pineapple Upside-Down Cake

makes 10 servings
ideal slow cooker: 4-quart

½ cup butter or margarine, melted
1 cup firmly packed brown sugar
20-oz. can pineapple slices,
  undrained
6 to 8 maraschino cherries
18.25-oz. pkg. yellow cake mix

1. Combine butter and brown sugar; spread over bottom of greased slow cooker.
2. Drain pineapple, reserving juice. Arrange pineapple slices and cherries in brown sugar mixture.
3. Prepare cake according to package directions, using pineapple juice for part of liquid. Spoon cake batter over fruit in slow cooker.
4. Cover slow cooker with 2 cotton kitchen towels and then with the slow cooker lid. Cook on high 1 hour. Turn heat to low and cook 3 to 4 hours more. Scoop cake from slow cooker into individual serving bowls.

Upside-Down Chocolate Pudding Cake

makes 8 servings
ideal slow cooker: 3½-quart

1 cup biscuit and baking mix (we used Bisquick)
1 cup sugar, divided
3 Tbsp. dry baking cocoa
½ cup milk
1 tsp. vanilla extract
⅓ cup dry baking cocoa
1⅔ cups hot water

1. Spray inside of slow cooker with cooking spray.
2. Combine baking mix, ½ cup sugar, 3 Tbsp. cocoa powder, milk, and vanilla in a mixing bowl, stirring until well blended. Spoon batter evenly into slow cooker.
3. Combine remaining ½ cup sugar, ⅓ cup cocoa powder, and hot water, stirring with a whisk until blended. Pour over batter in slow cooker. Do not stir.
4. Cover and cook on high 2 to 3 hours or until toothpick inserted in center of cake comes out clean.

tip:

• The batter will rise to the top and turn into cake. Underneath there will be a rich chocolate pudding.

---

5 ingredients or less

Brownies with Pecans

makes 24 brownies
ideal slow cooker: 5-quart

¼ cup butter, melted
1 cup chopped pecans, divided
23-oz. pkg. brownie mix

1. Pour melted butter into a baking insert designed to fit inside slow cooker. Swirl butter around to coat sides of insert.
2. Sprinkle butter with half the pecans.
3. Prepare brownie batter according to package directions. Spoon half the batter over pecans in baking insert. Sprinkle with remaining pecans. Carefully spread remaining batter over chopped pecans.
4. Place insert in slow cooker. Cover insert with 8 paper towels. Cover with slow cooker lid and cook on high 2 to 3 hours or until a toothpick inserted in the center comes out clean.
5. Let brownies stand at least 5 minutes before slicing.

serving tip:

• Slicing warm brownies with a disposable plastic knife rather than a stainless-steel knife makes brownie servings picture-perfect.

---

make-ahead

Triple Chocolate-Covered Peanut Clusters

makes about 5 dozen
ideal slow cooker: 4-quart

16-oz. jar dry-roasted peanuts
16-oz. jar unsalted dry-roasted peanuts
18 2-oz. chocolate bark coating squares, cut in half
12 ozs. semisweet chocolate morsels
4-oz. pkg. German chocolate baking squares, broken into pieces
9.75-oz. can salted whole cashews
1 tsp. vanilla extract

1. Combine first 5 ingredients in slow cooker. Cover and cook on low 2 hours or until chocolate is melted.
2. Stir mixture until smooth. Add cashews and vanilla, stirring well to coat cashews.
3. Drop nut mixture by heaping tablespoonfuls onto wax paper. Let stand until firm. Store in an airtight container at room temperature up to 2 weeks or in freezer up to a month.

index

favorite recipes

These recipes drew rave reviews in our
Test Kitchens, and they're the ones our staff whip up
for their own families and friends.

1 The Simplest "Baked" Potatoes, *page 19*

2 Fajita Steak, *page 21*

3 Chocolate Soufflé Cake, *page 35*

4 Crab Spread, *page 37*

5 Pizza Fondue, *page 47*

6 Hot Mint Malts, *page 58*

7 Chicken and Bean Torta, *page 79*

8 Winter Squash and White Bean Stew, *page 83*

9 Golden Cauliflower, *page 97*

10 Tex-Mex Shredded Pork Sandwiches, *page 64*